THE
BAUHAUS

STAATLICHES BAUHAUS

AUSSTELLUNG

JULI SEPT

WEIMAR

1923

THE BAUHAUS

Doreen Ehrlich

MAGNA BOOKS

Published by Magna Books
Magna Road
Wigston
Leicester LE8 2ZH

Produced by Bison Books Ltd.
Kimbolton House
117A Fulham Road
London SW3 6RL

ISBN 1-85422-133-7

Printed in Hong Kong

Page 1 The first Bauhaus
seal, 1919, designed by Karl-
Peter Röhl.
Kunstsammlungen zu
Weimar.

Page 2 Joost Schmidt,
Bauhaus Exhibition poster,
1923. Bauhaus Archiv, Berlin.

Contents

Introduction:
Origins and Antecedents

Wassily Kandinsky
Composition VIII 1923, oil on
canvas, 40½ inches × 78½
inches (104 × 201 cm).
Solomon R Guggenheim
Museum, New York, ©
ADAGP Paris and DACS
London 1991. Kandinsky was
one of the nine original
Masters of Form invited by
Walter Gropius to join the
Weimar Bauhaus.

The Bauhaus was not only the most famous art school of the twentieth century, it was also an idea: an idea that continues to influence all our lives. We live and work in buildings influenced by the Bauhaus, and use everyday objects such as metal reading lamps and chairs which had their origins in the Bauhaus workshops at Weimar and Dessau 70 years ago. The very layout and typography of today's books and magazines shows the mark of the Bauhaus, and its influence on the education of young artists and designers is incalculable. Many of the key figures of twentieth-century art and architecture, from the architect Walter Gropius, to whose vision and extraordinary skills it owed its existence, to the painters Paul Klee and Wassily Kandinsky, taught there. The architect and last Director, Ludwig Mies van der Rohe, writing some 20 years after the dissolution of the Bauhaus by the Nazis, defined the Bauhaus not as 'an institution – it was an idea . . . The fact that it was an idea is the cause of this enormous influence the Bauhaus had on every progressive school around the globe . . . Only an idea spreads so far . . .' The 'Bauhaus idea' was disseminated by its exiles, many of whom, like Mies and Gropius himself, were to occupy key posts in the United States.

In 1923 the painter and theatrical designer, Oskar Schlemmer, who was then teaching at the Bauhaus, wrote:

Four years of the Bauhaus reflect not only a period of art history but a history of the times too because the disintegration of a nation and of an era is also reflected in it,

thus affirming the idea of the *Zeitgeist*, 'spirit of the times'. The 14-year life of the Bauhaus spans, and is inextricably bound up with, the political, economic and cultural history of the extraordinarily brilliant period of the Weimar Republic, a period which first saw Bertolt Brecht and Kurt Weill's *The Threepenny Opera*, Expressionist films such as *The Cabinet of Dr Caligari*, the cartoons of Georg Grosz, Thomas Mann's *The Magic Mountain* and a galaxy of legendary figures which ranges from Albert Einstein to Marlene Dietrich. The Weimar Constitution and the Bauhaus were both founded in 1919 in the historic city of Goethe and Schiller, and were ended in Berlin in 1933 by Adolf Hitler, one of whose first acts of artistic policy was to close the Bauhaus, as a prime example of 'decadent' and 'Bolshevik' cultural activity.

The year of the founding of both the Weimar Republic and the Bauhaus, 1919 was a momentous one in the period of chaos in Germany after its defeat the year before in the First World War, 'the war to end all wars'. During the worst inflation Europe has ever known, the Bauhaus provided the first students with food (the canteen became the center of the school community) and shelter as well as their education, despite the terrible privations of the time. Many of the first students at Weimar had been on active service for the past four years, and their uniforms were in many cases their only clothing. These first students were drawn from all over Germany and some from abroad.

The radical education they were to receive was set down in the *Manifesto and Programme* published in April 1919, which attracted many students by its vision of the future at such a time. The words are those of Walter Gropius, first and greatest Director of the Bauhaus. The text is accompanied and reinforced by a full-page woodcut printed on yellow paper of a futuristic Gothic cathedral by Lyonel Feininger which echoes, in both its form and content, Gropius' vision of 'the crystal symbol of the new faith of the future'. The choice of woodcut as a technique is deliberately archaic, as used by such contemporary Expressionist groups as *Die Brücke* (The Bridge) and *Der Sturm* (The Storm) with which Feininger was associated. Its revival looked back to the medieval period when woodcut was used in Germany and the rest of Europe as a medium for popular prints and broadsheets. *Cathedral*, in its fusion of utopian ideals of the past and its future vision, is essentially Expressionist: powerful, dynamic and emotive.

The *Manifesto* begins with the declaration:

The complete building is the ultimate aim of the visual arts!
The highest function of the fine arts was once the decoration of buildings, and the fine arts were once indispensable to great architecture. Today they exist in complacent isolation, and can only be rescued by the joint conscious efforts of all craftsmen. Architects, painters and sculptors must once again come to know and understand the composite character of a building both as a whole and in terms of the sum of its parts. Only then will their works be filled with that true architectonic spirit which has become lost in the art of the salons.

Below Ludwig Mies van der Rohe, Weissenhof chair, c.1927, tubular steel and wicker. Courtesy of the Trustees of the Victoria and Albert Museum. Already an internationally renowned architect, Mies became Director of the Dessau Bauhaus in 1930.

Opposite Lyonel Feininger *Cathedral* 1919, woodcut. Bauhaus Archiv, Berlin, © COSMOPRESS Geneva and DACS London 1991. Title page of the *Bauhaus Manifesto*, for which Walter Gropius wrote the text.

Thus the visual arts were to be saved from what was seen as their crippling isolation, and artists and craftsmen were to work in co-operation, one with another on the ultimate aim of all creative activity, 'the complete building of the future', the total work of art. The term *Bauhaus* is untranslatable; '*bau*' in German literally means 'construction' as well as 'building'. In the Middle Ages, evoked in both word and image in the *Manifesto*, the *Bauhütten* were the guilds associated with building crafts. The Bauhaus was not literally to be a school for builders, but rather an exclusive community for the training of creatively skilled craftworkers who, by working on collaborative projects, were to have their characters shaped both by the training and the community of which they were part. Gropius hoped that his school would act as a catalyst of social change through design, just as the Expressionist artists of the immediate post-war years believed that art could change society.

Secondly the *Manifesto* urges a return to the system of crafts that prevailed in the Middle Ages, before the Renaissance saw the elevation of the status of artists.

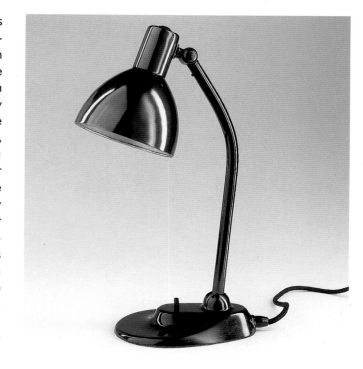

Architects, painters, sculptors we must all return to the crafts! For there is no such thing as 'professional art'. There is no essential difference between the artist and the craftsman: the artist is a craftsman raised to a higher power. In rare moments of illumination, which transcend the will, the Grace of Heaven may cause his handiwork to flower into art, but a foundation of craft-discipline is essential to every artist..

Let us therefore create a new guild of craftsmen, without the class-distinction that tries to erect an arrogant barrier between craftsman and artist. Let us conceive, consider and create together the new building of the future that will bring everything into one single integrated creation: architecture, painting and sculpture rising to Heaven out of the hands of a million craftsmen, the crystal symbol of the new faith of the future.

The 'crystal symbol' was powerfully signified by Feininger's woodcut and by the first Bauhaus signet, designed in medieval style to show a symbolic building being raised by the craftsman-artists. Gropius' vision of 1919 was to have at least partial realization in his design for the buildings of the Dessau Bauhaus, which were equipped entirely with the products of the Bauhaus' own workshops. Gropius' opening speech in December 1926 echoed something of his earlier idealism in his hope that the School would prove to be 'a spiritual center for all our young people'.

In the Bauhaus *Manifesto* of 1919, utopian medievalism, which played such an important part in Gropius' thinking at this time, also informs the concept of there being 'no teachers or pupils at the Bauhaus' but a workshop system following the guild practice of 'masters, journeymen and apprentices'. Manual skills could be taught in such a workshop system, which was the first principle of the Bauhaus method from the beginning. This training (which was to be subject to examination at 'journeyman standard' by the State Chamber of Handicrafts) was to be combined with the school training in an understanding of medium, form and color. However, this far-reaching concept was not hierarchical: the *Programme* states, 'The school is the servant of the workshop and will one day be absorbed by it'.

Gropius hoped to ensure economic freedom for the State Bauhaus at some future date, hence the emphasis

should be remembered, however, that Gropius was an ex-cavalry officer and had, like many of his generation throughout Europe, been forced to change his views on the power of the machine by the unprecedented devastation of the First World War.

The need for a radical change in art and craft education was under discussion even before the war. Germany's embattled economy demanded an increase in trained designers to enable industrial concerns to increase the export of manufactured goods of all kinds.

While the Weimar School of Arts and Crafts was closed during the war, Gropius was approached with a view to redesigning the educational programme for the new post-war generation of designers so vital to Germany's economic recovery. He was given permission to name the institution, of which he was the first Director, the State Bauhaus. Despite the ringing tones of the *Manifesto*, the merger of two incompatible entities, the Weimar Academy of Fine Art, founded in 1860, and the School of Arts and Crafts, caused considerable difficulties, particularly as Gropius inherited four orthodox professors from the former Academy as well as a full complement of their students.

These students were now termed apprentices and journeymen, their studios became workshops and they were no longer permitted to extend their education indefinitely, as had been the practice in the past. The Bauhaus training was to be of four years' duration, and the crafts-based nature of the training was further reinforced by the tutors, and indeed professors, being termed Masters. Before tracing the story of the Bauhaus' first years at Weimar, however, it is important to establish a context for the State Bauhaus in the wider history of European design, as well as looking more closely at the German context.

The exhibition held in London in 1851, The Great Exhibition of the Works of Industry of all Nations, the first of all such international exhibitions, provides a useful

Below The Machinery Court at the Great Exhibition, Crystal Palace, London, 1851.

in the *Programme* on the need to 'establish constant contact with the leaders of the crafts and industries of the country'. To modern eyes, one of several puzzling omissions in the 1919 *Manifesto and Programme* is any mention of machine production, curious indeed from an architect with Gropius' reputation as one of Germany's leading exponents of the New Architecture. It

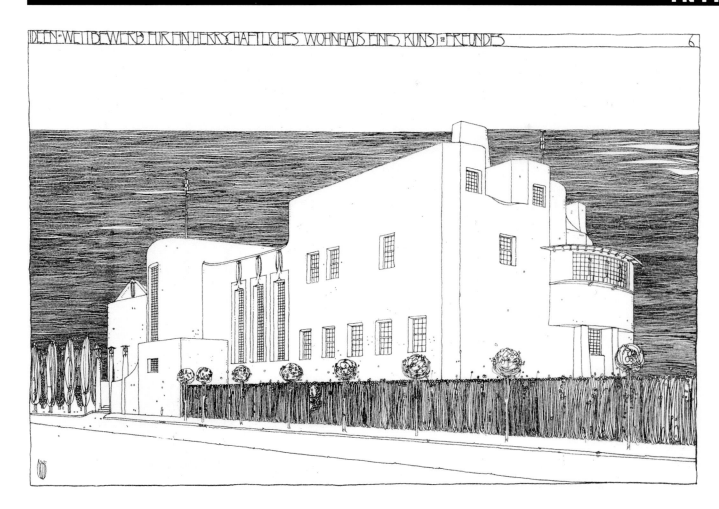

IDEEN·WETTBEWERB·FUR·EIN·HERRSCHAFTLICHES·WOHNHAUS·EINES·KUNST·FREUNDES

Left Charles Rennie Mackintosh, House for a Lover of Art, perspective from the north-west, 1901. Hunterian Art Gallery, University of Glasgow. Mackintosh produced the design for a German competition.

Below William Morris, Sussex armchair, 1860s. William Morris Gallery, London. This rush-seated armchair is characteristic of the traditionally handcrafted objects produced by the firm of Morris, Marshall, Faulkner and Co.

starting point for a consideration of the origins of Gropius' idea of the Bauhaus. The radical iron and glass pre-fabricated structure which housed the Great Exhibition, popularly dubbed The Crystal Palace, was to anticipate all such buildings in later nineteenth- and early twentieth-century architecture, including Gropius' own. The exhibits from manufacturers from all over the world (including incidentally, Gropius' great uncle, who won a medal) were a heterogeneous mix of fine art, new machinery and the products that could be produced by such machines.

The Master of Trinity College, Cambridge, lecturing in November 1851, spoke for many visitors: 'Britain supplies the wants of the many . . . the machine with its million fingers works for millions of purchasers'. Others, including the most influential critic of the time, John Ruskin, were more concerned with production than consumption. Ruskin saw the technological advances demonstrated in the Great Exhibition and the division of the labor process as degrading the value of work and destroying individuality. He particularly disliked the use of materials such as papier mâché to simulate wood; 'Whatever the material you choose to work with, your art is base if it does not bring out the distinctive qualities of that material'. Ruskin also founded the Guild of St George in 1872, aiming to reform society by a return to the medieval guild system, which directly influenced Walter Gropius' idea of the Bauhaus. Although the Guild of St George soon foundered, it was the prototype for such later successful groups as the Art Workers' Guild, founded in 1884 and still in existence, and the Guild of Handicraft, founded 1888 by the designer C R Ashbee, whose work, along with that of the designer-architect Charles Rennie Mackintosh, was highly influential both at home and abroad.

Ruskin's younger contemporary, William Morris, was to prove most influential on Bauhaus ideas, and

indeed on the whole course of twentieth-century design. Morris, designer, poet, socialist and master of many crafts, also wrote of the importance of 'truth to material' and abhorred mechanization. He endeavored to raise the status of the craftsworker; 'Why in the name of patience should a craftsman be a worse gentleman than a lawyer?' His firm, Morris, Marshall, Faulkner and Co advertised itself in its first prospectus of 1861 as Fine Art Workmen in Painting, Carving, Furniture and the Metals, yet the traditionally handcrafted objects produced by the Firm were ironically affordable only by the few. Morris's utopian socialism extended to a desire to return to the conditions of the medieval past: an imagined past, a time, as he conceived it, of the wholeness of art, morality of politics and religion, dignity of labor. The forms of Morris' designs for such household objects as chairs and settles and indeed for larger public projects were drawn from the Middle Ages, and private purchasers were exhorted to 'have nothing in your homes that you do not know to be useful or believe to be beautiful'. This reaction of Morris, the central figure of the Arts and Crafts Movement, to the Machine Age was influential both in Great Britain and abroad.

Also highly influential was the idea of the total work of art, exemplified by such a setpiece as the Morris Room at the Victoria and Albert Museum, London, where the furniture, wall treatments and stained glass were designed by Morris and his fellow workers. How-

ever great the influence of Morris, the turn-of-the-century integration of architecture, interior design, and furniture and fittings into the total work of art which perhaps most influenced contemporary German design was the Scottish architect Charles Rennie Mackintosh's project for the competition organized by the interior design periodical *Zeitschrift für Innendekoration* in 1901.

Mackintosh, architect and designer of the Glasgow School of Art, whose work was to have greater resonance on the continent than in Britain, produced for the 'House for a Lover of Art' design brief a novel treatment of his declared belief that 'construction should be decorated, and not decoration constructed . . . the salient and most requisite features should be selected for ornamentation'. These ideas can be seen both in the facade of the house and in the design of the music room, where the decorative panels, designed by Margaret Macdonald, Mackintosh's wife, take a lyre as their motif, which is repeated throughout the room including the spectacular light fittings. Mackintosh's entry was published as a portfolio in 1902 in *Meister der Innenkunst* (Masters of Interior Design) with an introduction by the architect Hermann Muthesius (1861-1927), an admirer of British architecture and design.

Muthesius had spent seven years in Britain in a specially created post as a German government trade attaché, to report on British architecture, design and housing policy and the teaching methods employed in

Below Charles Rennie Mackintosh and Margaret Macdonald, Music Room, from the House for a Lover of Art. Hunterian Art Gallery, University of Glasgow.

the training of architects and designers. His hugely influential three-volume *Das Englische Haus* (The English House, published in 1904 and 1905) was thoroughgoing in its examination not only of middle-class domestic architecture and design but also of such utilities as plumbing. Muthesius was much influenced by such English ideas as 'truth to materials' but also sought what he termed 'modern means' to meet the modern needs of all classes. Such modern means involved machine production and the 'children of the new age', the industrialist and the engineer. When, on his return to Germany, Muthesius was appointed to the post of Superintendent of the schools of arts and crafts in Prussia, the English workshop training method of 'learning by doing' was introduced throughout the country.

Perhaps the greatest contribution to German design in the period immediately before the First World War, however, was the Deutscher Werkbund set up in 1907, primarily by Muthesius. The Werkbund was an association of twelve leading artists and twelve industrialists, whose declared aim was to improve the design and manufacture of German goods. In the first seven years of its existence Muthesius was the most influential figure in the Werkbund. The society aimed to foster 'the best in art, industry, craftsmanship and trade' and to help join 'all those efforts to achieve quality that is evident in all industrial endeavor'. The English origin of such a concept of an industrial design society can be

Above Peter Behrens, electric kettle, 1908. Courtesy of the Trustees of the British Museum, © DACS 1991. Peter Behrens was appointed architect and chief designer to the German company AEG in 1907; the kettle is one of many products he designed in this capacity.

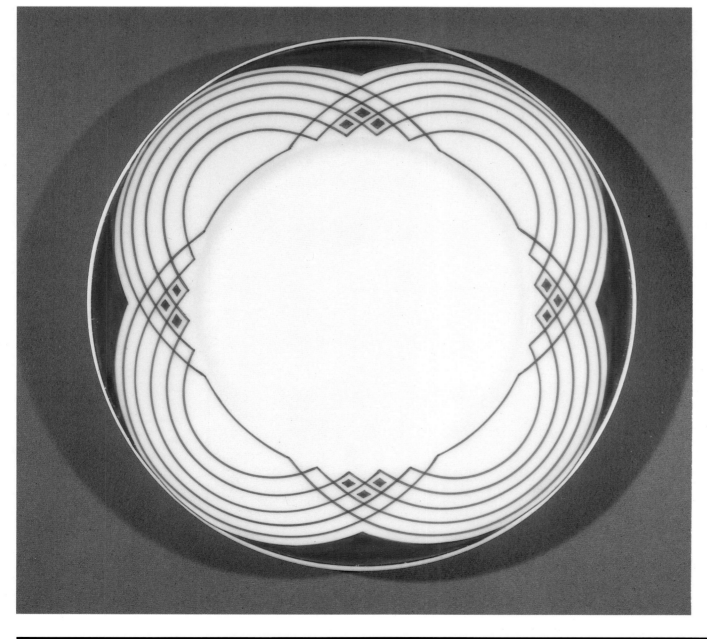

Left Peter Behrens, plate designed for Bamscher, Weiden, c.1901. Courtesy of the Trustees of the British Museum, © DACS 1991.

Left Walter Gropius and Adolf Meyer, office building designed for the Cologne Werkbund Exhibition, 1914. Bauhaus Archiv, Berlin. Gropius became a member of the Deutscher Werkbund, a formative influence on the Bauhaus, in 1912. After the exhibition closed all the buildings on the site were demolished.

Right Bruno Taut, Glass Pavilion designed for the Deutscher Werkbund Exhibition in Cologne, 1914. Taut was one of several Werkbund members who designed buildings in a more or less Expressionist style. Many of the artists whom Gropius brought to Weimar had similarly Expressionist connections.

Below Walter Gropius and Adolf Meyer, Fagus shoe-last factory, Alfeld-an-der-Leine, 1910-11. Bauhaus Archiv, Berlin. This startlingly original use of glass and steel is early evidence of Gropius' revolutionary rethinking of modern constructional technique.

Right Lászlo Moholy-Nagy, cover design for *Holländische Architektur* by J-J P Oud, volume ten in the Bauhaus Books series. Bauhaus Archiv, Berlin. Moholy-Nagy joined the Bauhaus in 1923, replacing Johannes Itten.

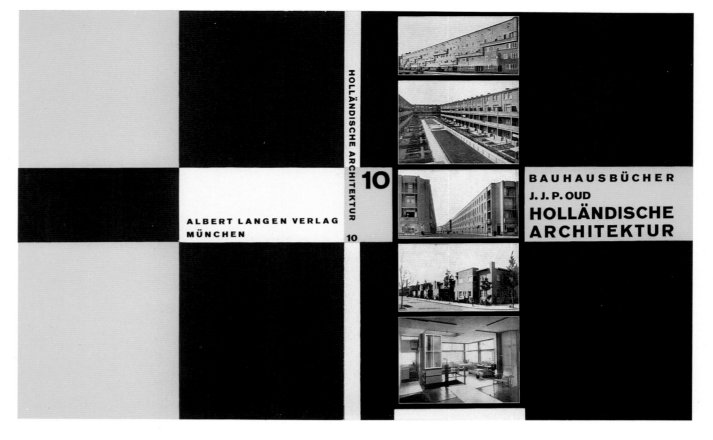

Below Henry van de Velde, Weimar Academy of Art, 1904-10. The work of the Belgian artist van de Velde, a member of the Deutscher Werkbund, was influential on the Bauhaus. He became Director of the Weimar Academy of Applied Arts in 1901, and from 1919 his academy building became the first home of the Bauhaus.

seen in the fact that the word 'design' had to be appropriated from English as no German equivalent existed.

In the same year as the founding of the Werkbund, one of its leading members, the architect Peter Behrens, who was to employ Le Corbusier as well as Gropius and Mies van der Rohe as assistants in his private architectural practice, was appointed as Architect and Chief Designer to the Allgemeine Elektrizitäts Gellschaft or AEG, the German general electricity company and one of the country's most important industrial concerns. Behrens was to design many of AEG's buildings, the most famous of which was the electricity company's turbine construction hall in Berlin. Even more important was the fact that Behrens was responsible for the design of all the company's products, from street lamps to electric kettles and even to their catalogue and stationery, thus establishing an early form of corporate identity. There were three years of Werkbund *Yearbooks*, containing a record of the achievement of the society. Apart from Behrens' own work, which included designs for the AEG showrooms, the achievement of the Werkbund can be gauged by the designs for mass production by Richard Riemerschmid, from metalwork to linoleum and furniture. Gropius, who was to join Behrens' architectural practice soon after the latter's appointment to AEG, wrote of his association with the older architect in *The New Architecture and the Bauhaus* (1935):

In the course of my active association in the important schemes on which he was engaged . . . my own ideas began to crystallize as to what the essential nature of a building ought to be . . . modern constructional technique could not be denied expression in architecture and that expression demanded the use of unprecedented forms.

Walter Gropius (1883-1969) was born into a family of architects and educators and trained in Berlin and Munich before beginning work as Behrens' assistant in 1907, the year of the founding of the Werkbund. By 1910 he had set up in partnership with Adolf Meyer and two of the buildings they produced, the Fagus shoe-last factory in Alfeld (a small town near Hildesheim) and a small model factory for the Werkbund Exhibition in Cologne of 1914, were startlingly original in their use of glass and steel, evidence indeed of Gropius' rethinking of 'modern constructional technique . . . and . . . the use of unprecedented forms', as he was later to express it. The Werkbund factory was also remarkable for its glass facade, which exemplified the importance Gropius placed on transparency, enabling utilities such as the staircases to be seen. Gropius became a member of the Werkbund in 1912, not only designing buildings such as the Cologne exhibition factory but, as was the practice for group members, also designing various items of domestic furniture and fittings, a diesel engine, and the fixtures and fittings of a railway sleeping car.

Another member of the Werkbund whose work was to have a lasting influence on both Gropius and the Bauhaus was the Belgian artist, architect and designer, Henry van de Velde (1863-1957). Van de Velde, who changed the spelling of his first name to the English form as a response to the fashion for the English Arts and Crafts Movement which swept Europe at the turn of the century, was the leading Belgian designer of his day. In 1900 van de Velde moved to Berlin and a year later he was appointed Director of the Weimar Academy of Applied Arts. In Weimar van de Velde had the official task of providing through the Arts and Crafts Seminar 'artistic inspiration to craftsmen and industrialists by producing designs, models, examples and so forth'.

Van de Velde was a founder member of the Werkbund and in 1914, at the time of the Cologne exhibition, he and Gropius opposed Muthesius, who proposed the use of standardized 'norms' in architecture and design throughout Germany in a public debate on the subject. Gropius' debt to the Belgian was considerable. Van de Velde proposed him as the first Director of the amalgamated Weimar Academy of Fine Art and the School of Arts and Crafts – from which post van de Velde, as an enemy alien, had been forced to resign on the outbreak of hostilities. In 1924, in his early essay *Concept and Development of the State Bauhaus*, Gropius writes that the Bauhaus was indebted to:

Ruskin and Morris in England, van de Velde in Belgium, Behrens . . . and others in Germany, and finally the German Werkbund . . . (all) consciously sought and found the first ways to the reuniting of the working world and that of creative artists.

The Cologne Werkbund Exhibition, which opened in July 1914, was prematurely closed on the outbreak of war in August 1914; the exhibition halls were converted into makeshift space to receive the first of the wounded soldiers from the front. The buildings designed by van de Velde and Gropius, together with others specially built for the exhibition, were destroyed within a few months.

Among them was a curious Expressionist building by the visionary Werkbund member, Bruno Taut. The domed Glass Pavilion, built for the glass industry and intended as a demonstration setpiece for the material, was built of glass bricks and panes, many of different colors. The interior staircase of glass treads and risers was surmounted by a tall glass geodesic dome. Taut conceived architecture as a vehicle for social change, as did the fantasy-fiction writer Paul Scheerbart whose

novel *Glasarchitektur* (published in 1914) was dedicated to Taut. Scheerbart conceived a utopian city of the future built of glass: 'Glass brings us the new Age / Brick-culture does us nothing but harm'. The dome of Taut's Glass Pavilion was inscribed with such specially written legends by Scheerbart as 'Colored glass destroys hatred'. The synthesis in one architectural structure of utopian and futuristic concepts, together with ideas related to Gothic theories of transparency and truth, is in a similar Expressionist vein to Feininger's *Cathedral* and indeed evokes something of the tone of Gropius' Bauhaus *Manifesto*.

Gropius was to seek to change the social consciousness of his students through the collaborative venture of the Bauhaus programme. The early years of the Bauhaus at Weimar owe much to ideas which can loosely be called Expressionist rather than for example to the ideas of Peter Behrens, who sought to achieve a synthesis of mechanized production and the craftsman's skills, or of van de Velde, who expressed the ideal state for his own designs as being 'the thousandfold multiplication of my creations'.

Above Lou Scheper, typographical collage, c.1927. Courtesy of Barry Friedman Ltd. Typical of the innovative graphic and typographical work carried out in the graphics workshop, this was a student tribute to the artist and Bauhaus tutor Florence Henri, whose name appears top right.

The Early Years of the Weimar Bauhaus

Walter Gropius had begun negotiations for a reformed arts and crafts curriculum with the authorities in Weimar well before the First World War. He had delivered a paper as early as 1916 outlining his proposals for the remodelling of the courses at the School of Arts and Crafts. This proposed a 'partnership between the artist, industrialist and technician, who, organized in keeping with the spirit of the times, might perhaps eventually be in a position to replace all the factors of the old, individual work'. Gropius served as a cavalry officer during the war and saw action at the devastating Battle of the Somme in 1917, where he was badly wounded, being twice awarded the order of the Iron Cross. Little else is known of the details of his war service but it is certain that the seminal experience shaped his future ideas. As he himself put it in an address to the Bauhaus students in July 1919 at the first exhibition of their work:

We are in the midst of a monstrous catastrophe in the history of the world, of a transformation of all of life and of the *entire* inner being ... Those who experienced (the war) out there have come back completely changed; they see that things cannot continue in the old ways.

Gropius explained the choice of the historic city of Weimar to the Director of the Weimar Theater, Ernst Hardt, less than a week after he had been appointed Director of the Weimar Academy of Fine Art and officially allowed to merge the Academy with the School for Arts and Crafts:

My idea of Weimar is not a small one ... I firmly believe that Weimar, precisely because it is world-famous, is the best place to lay the foundation stone of a republic of intellects.

Weimar, as the seat of the Thuringian government, was at the cutting edge of events in such troubled times; less than a year later a group of strikers was shot dead in the city. Their monument was commissioned by the Weimar trades unions from the Bauhaus after several projected designs had been submitted. Gropius' dynamic design for the *Monument to the March Heroes* was executed in concrete in the Bauhaus stone carving workshop. It evokes in three dimensions some of the Expressionist qualities of Feininger's *Manifesto* woodcut *Cathedral*, with its echoes of both futuristic crystal structures and the spires of the great Gothic cathedrals. Badly damaged in the Nazi period, it has now been restored to its previous powerful dramatic form in the cemetery at Weimar.

Gropius' current political sympathies were embodied in the monument; the architect of the Bauhaus proclamation rather than that of the functionalist Fagus factory is evident here. The same vein is explored in his vision of the future presented to the Bauhaus students at the first exhibition of their work in July 1919:

What will develop are not large intellectual institutions but small, secret, closed associations ... which preserve ... a secret core of belief until a general, great, productive, intellectual and religious idea emerges from the individual groupings, an idea which must ultimately find its expression crystallized in a great, total work of art. And this cathedral ... of the future will illuminate the smallest things of everyday life with floods of light.

The first Bauhaus students who enrolled with such high hopes in the year following Germany's defeat in the war were in need of every reassurance. They came from all over Germany and there were some students from Hungary and several from Austria. Most of them were in their early 20s, although some were as young as 17 and there were some mature students nearing 40. Two thirds were men and at least half of that number had served in the war. Most were in need of such basic material provision as food and shelter, and many faced their school day already tired by working in local factories for small sums of money, the value of which was further eroded by raging post-war inflation. The school set up a canteen, which was essential to the material welfare of both students and staff, providing food – partly grown in the Bauhaus market garden – and an essential focus for social activity. Many students were inadequately clothed and Gropius arranged for the supply of essentials where this was possible. Several students adapted uniforms by dyeing and creative stitchery, setting themselves apart from the citizens of Weimar by their bizarre clothing.

More serious than the privations of student life for the future of the Bauhaus was the shortage of essential workshop equipment. After Germany's defeat in the war, administrative and economic chaos reigned throughout the country. Weimar, which became the

capital of the federal Thuringian state in 1920, was no exception in its administrative problems or in its lack of public funds. The dire straits of the Bauhaus can be gauged by Gropius' impassioned plea in March 1920 to the Thuringian Ministry of Education and Justice, now responsible for the administration of public monies:

We cannot work without materials and tools! If help does not speedily arrive I think the future existence of the Bauhaus is in doubt. Many must leave the school or want to leave it because they are unable to work.

Compounding Gropius' difficulties in the first year of the Bauhaus was the hostile attitude of the so-called Weimar Citizens' Committee which saw the Bauhaus as a dangerous Communist-dominated institution, infiltrated by Jews and non-Germans. In response Gropius stated that the students were all German-speaking, of German origin, and that 'only 17 [of a student body of some 217] were of Jewish extraction of whom none has a grant and most have been baptised . . . [all the others] are Aryans'. Some of the more conservative elements from the former Academy of Fine Art were also opposed to the new regime. The traditional painters and sculptors, both staff and students, eventually, and perhaps inevitably, broke away and became re-established as a separate institution again in September 1920, when the former Academy teachers left the Bauhaus, taking 28 of their students with them. That the Bauhaus survived its first year was a tribute to Gropius' extraordinary powers as an administrator and a tribute too to the support given him by the Ministry of Culture in Weimar, which was socialist until 1924. Gropius' belief that the training of artists and craftsmen should be one

Right Lyonel Feininger *Cats* 1921, woodcut. Courtesy of the Trustees of the British Museum, © COSMOPRESS Geneva and DACS London 1991. Feininger was one of the nine original Masters of Form appointed by Gropius to the Weimar Bauhaus between 1919 and 1924.

Below Georg Muche *Stilleben aus Glas* 1920/21, still-life photograph. Bauhaus Archiv, Berlin. Muche, an Expressionist painter who had exhibited with *Der Sturm* in Berlin, became Master of Form in the weaving workshop and Itten's assistant on the *Vorkurs*.

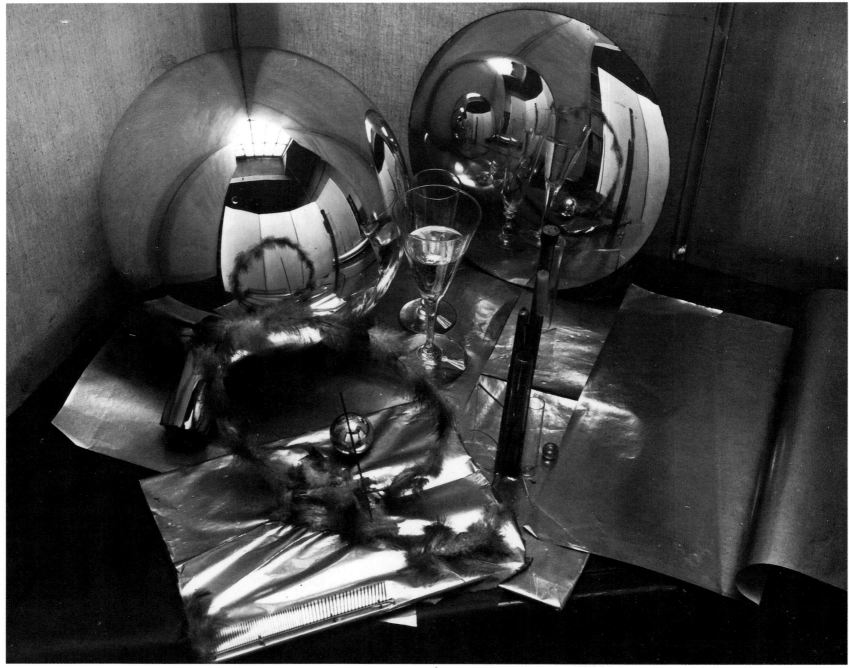

and the same — an introduction to the basic components of form, color and the nature of materials — was the cornerstone of the teaching of the first years at Weimar. He structured the Bauhaus teaching programme on the belief that there was little fundamental difference between the activities of art and craft, rather that each was a variant of the other.

The appointment of the first Masters of Form at Weimar can only be understood in these terms. In the years between 1919 and 1924, of the nine Masters of Form appointed, no less than eight were painters, the ninth being the sculptor and printmaker Gerhard Marcks. Although the work of each of these already well-known artists was very different (the work of such painters as Feininger and Kandinsky can only be very loosely linked as Expressionist), all the Masters could translate their experience as painters, practised in such fundamentals as form and color, into their teaching practice. All nine were impressive appointments: Gropius had been highly selective in choosing artists with ideals and the Masters were remarkable not only for their varying artistic achievements but for the skill with which they could communicate their ideas to others. This quality is a far from common characteristic in artists, however distinguished; words are often blunt instruments when used to communicate ideas expressed in another medium. The nine original Masters of Form, Paul Klee, Wassily Kandinsky, Lyonel Feininger, Gerhard Marcks, Lothar Schreyer, Georg Muche, Oskar Schlemmer, Johannes Itten and Lázló Moholy-Nagy, might have known very little about the technicalities of weaving or metalwork, but Gropius saw them working alongside their Craft Master equivalents creating a productive and exciting dynamic by such dual instruction. Gropius claimed to be 'training the architects of a new civilization'. Writing in *The New Architecture* in 1935, he explained:

That was why we made it a rule in the Bauhaus that every pupil and apprentice had to be taught throughout by two masters working in the closest collaboration with each other; and that no pupil or apprentice could be excused from attending the classes of either. The Practical Instruction was the most important part of our preparation for collective work and also the most effective way of combatting artycrafty tendencies.

JOHANNES ITTEN
AND THE BASIC COURSE

Very few of the artists appointed as new Masters of Form had experience of teaching students. The most experienced teacher was Johannes Itten (1888-1967), whose four years at the Bauhaus left an indelible mark. During his first two years Itten wielded considerable power; Gropius allowed him to teach as Master of Form in more workshops than any of the other tutors and, at Itten's suggestion, the teaching of the all-important preliminary course was his responsibility alone. The six-month *Vorkurs* was the cornerstone of Bauhaus teaching in the early years and Itten decided who should take part in it, and by extension who should join the Bauhaus itself on satisfactorily completing the *Vorkurs*.

Itten was born in Switzerland and trained as a teacher of young children in the Froebel method, which advocated the practice of 'learning by doing' for the

Left Johannes Itten in the monastic robe he designed for himself. Bauhaus Archiv, Berlin. Itten belonged to the mystical cult of Mazdaznan, which advocated mental and physical discipline in pursuit of a higher reality.

very young. He decided to become a painter relatively late in his career, after studying mathematics and science, and attended the Academy at Stuttgart where he was taught by the radical abstract painter Adolf Hoelzel. Itten was running his own highly unconventional school in Vienna by 1916 and exhibiting with the Expressionist group *Der Sturm* when Alma Mahler

Below Vincent Weber *Study of Materials* 1920/21. Bauhaus Archiv, Berlin. One of the exercises on Itten's *Vorkurs* designed to identify the students' affinities with different materials.

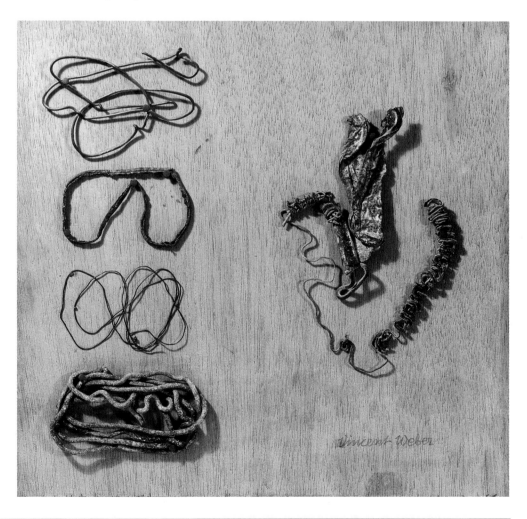

Klee joined the Bauhaus in 1920 at the age of 41, the same year that the first important exhibition of his work was held. He was involved with both the bookbinding and the stained-glass workshops but his most significant immediate contribution was to the *Vorkurs*. Later he also became involved with the weaving workshop, where he gave special classes on formal composition.

introduced him to her husband, Walter Gropius. He was at this time part of an avant-garde artistic and musical circle which included the artist Oskar Kokoschka, the designer Adolf Loos, who organized an exhibition of Itten's paintings in Vienna in 1919, and also the composer Arnold Schoenberg.

Itten was a mystic, a follower of the cult of Mazdaz-nan which derived from the ancient (Egyptian) cult of Zoroastrianism. This was the major pre-Islamic cult of Iran, which also had a considerable influence on Judaism and Christianity. The followers of Mazdaznan believe that what is usually perceived as the reality of the material world obscures a higher reality, for which the earthly body must be prepared by abstinence and

fasting and the mind by a series of rigorous mental exercises. Itten believed that there was innate creativity in each of his students, which would be released in the newly receptive body purged by following the rigorous mental and physical regime advocated by the Mazdanan cult. Itten and those of his students who followed the cult (including many of Itten's 16 students from his school in Vienna, who formed the nucleus of the first course at Dessau) ate only vegetarian food; indeed at one time the macrobiotic diet advocated by the cult was the only food served in the Bauhaus canteen. The male students shaved their heads and wore simple robes, and the female students wore short practical skirts and had their hair cut short. Itten's students and

Above Johannes Itten *A Group of Houses in Spring* 1916, oil on canvas, 35 × 29 inches (90 × 75 cm). Thyssen-Bornemisza Foundation, Lugano, © COSMOPRESS Geneva and DACS London 1991.

Right Plan of the training programme at Weimar. Kunstsammlungen zu Weimar. The outer edge of the wheel shows the half-year *Vorkurs*, then comes the study of materials and tools, geometry, color, composition, etc. The innermost circle represents color, textiles, glass, clay, stone, wood, metal, while the hub of the wheel is 'Building' – construction and engineering, building site, testing site and design.

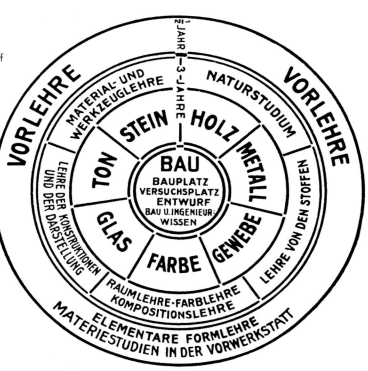

their charismatic tutor were thus set apart from the rest of the Bauhaus. Their bizarre appearance was, however, only the outward sign of Itten's extraordinary influence on their development.

Itten was later to write that what had most attracted him to the Bauhaus were the classrooms and workshops; he also mentioned the fact that 'the premises were still empty and new facilities could be installed without much demolition'. As it turned out, there were very few resources available in the first years and even basic necessities like looms were scarce; on one level Itten's Basic Course may be seen as a triumph of invention over dire necessity. Of much greater significance than his statement above is Itten's later declaration '... generously, Walter Gropius left me a completely free hand in its (the Basic Course's) arrangement and content'. He had three aims in the Basic Course (or *Vorkurs*) as he insisted on calling it, rather than Preliminary Course, as it was later termed. The first task as Itten saw it was to free 'the creativity present in every student'; in the process his students would be able to 'rid themselves of the dead wood of

Right Willi Dieckmann, study of materials from Ittens' *Vorkurs*, 1920/21. Bauhaus Archiv, Berlin. These exercises were designed to develop a tactile sense and an understanding of the qualities of different materials.

convention and acquire the courage to create their own work'.

The second aim was to make the students' choice of career easier by discovering their several affinities to various materials. This was done by encouraging them to work with clay, wood, metal and textiles, so that each student discovered the medium 'that inspired him most' in Itten's words 'to creative work'. The third of Itten's aims was to present the students with the principles of creative composition for their future careers as artists. The Basic Course lasted one term and those who graduated from it were enabled both to proceed to the specialist workshops and, as Itten himself puts it,

'to prepare for future co-operation with industry'.

The course was designed as a trial period for students from varying backgrounds. The first students were a particularly disparate group. Itten had inherited some students trained in the conventions of academic art or traditional craft, and these had to be accommodated alongside the 16 students trained in Itten's methods who had come with him from Vienna.

Later a refined version of the syllabus was expressed in the famous 'wheel diagram', which showed the six-month basic course with its 'elementary study of form and study of materials' in the preliminary workshop, leading to the three-year course, which began with

Above left M Mirkin, study of materials from Ittens' *Vorkurs*, 1920/21. Bauhaus Archiv, Berlin. Here different materials – wood, iron, glass – and forms of expression – smooth, serrated, varying rhythms – are contrasted.

Above right Martin Jahn, rhythmical study from Ittens' *Vorkurs*, 1921, charcoal and pencil. Bauhaus Archiv, Berlin. This reflects Itten's policy of emphasizing particular aspects of a given motif.

such elements as 'study of equipment and tools, study of construction and representation, space and color study, study of composition and nature study'. The inner spokes of the wheel and the later stages of the course included more specialized work in the student's chosen medium; stone, wood, metal, textiles, glass, clay. The hub of the wheel was building design. Itten was to open the first exhibition of his students' work at the Bauhaus in 1918 by quoting the Chinese philosopher Lao-Tse: 'Thirty spokes meet in the hub, but the empty spaces between them are the essence of the wheel'.

Itten explained his interest in Eastern philosophy as a reaction to the terrible effects of the war.

I realized that outward-looking scientific research and technology must be balanced by inward-looking thinking and by our spiritual resources.

Accordingly each day's work on the Basic Course began with a series of breathing exercises and the

Above Peter Keler, cradle, 1922, painted wood and metal. Kunstsammlungen zu Weimar. The cradle, with its basic geometrical forms and primary colors, is a literal interpretation of the color theory developed first by Itten and then by Kandinsky on the *Vorkurs*.

Right Max Peiffer Watenphul, color study for Ittens' *Vorkurs*, 1920, collage of colored paper. Bauhaus Archiv, Berlin.

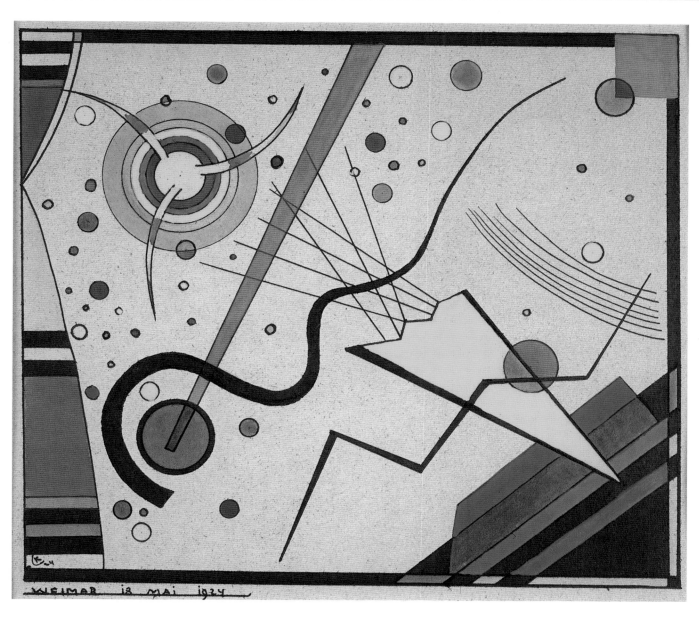

body and mind was prepared for the tasks of the day. Itten was adapting techniques he had used with young children of 'learning through play' which owed a great deal to the teachings of Froebel. As early as 1825 Froebel introduced nursery-age children to what he described as 'the divine unity' by allowing them to play only with cones, cubes and cylinders. In his school in Vienna Itten had also built on Maria Montessori's theories of 'learning by doing' by applying her methods to the teaching of art and design. The *Vorkurs* students were to experience a refined version of Itten's early methods, which included the 'experiencing' of basic geometrical forms in gesture before they were visually communicated to paper or modeled in clay. Itten was concerned that 'contrasts such as smooth/ rough, hard/soft, light/heavy' had to be felt as well as seen, and that each element should be perceived as part of a whole, not in isolation one from another.

When studies from this part of the course were exhibited as part of the students' work on the Basic Course, the assemblages caused some confusion and not a little outrage among visitors. The three-dimensional studies caused particular affront. Visitors to the first exhibition perceived such exercises as Herger's three-dimensional study in wood, glass and metal, with its contrasts of materials, textures and triangular, rectangular, circular, and cylindrical forms, not as an exercise but as a form of deliberately outrageous Dadaist sculpture, not a means to an end but an end in itself.

Itten's analytical exercises were similarly misunderstood. Analyses such as the well known deconstruction

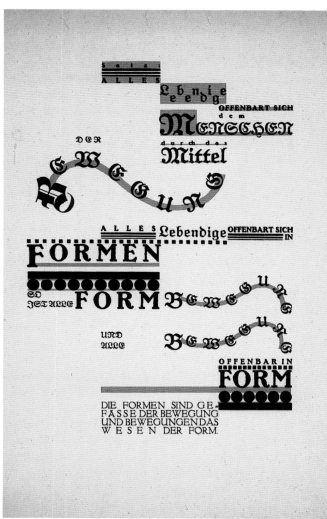

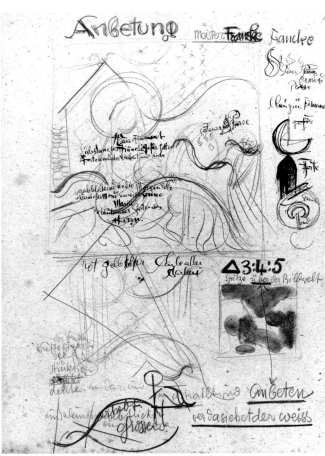

of the medieval German painter Meister Francke's *Adoration of the Magi* appeared to approximate to a common type of conventional art-historical analysis of formal values, by breaking down a painting in terms of line, form, etc. However Itten was concerned with other values, and his diagrams (originally published in *Utopia* in Weimar in 1921) show that he was interested in such underlying concepts as rhythmical analysis, the significance of various colors used in the painting, and the ways in which such qualities contribute to the painting's meaning.

Studies made directly from nature were an essential part of the Basic Course. Again these were not seen as an end in themselves but as part of the all-important process of learning how to see. This training of the eye was extended from an initial study of plants, which were not approached with a view merely to accurately depicting their botanical structure, but in terms of their underlying rhythm and forms. Similarly, life-drawing classes were conducted with strict regard not to anatomical precision but to the rhythm of various movements and their characteristic expression. To this end music was often played to the students as they worked, and what were perceived (in a variant of Gestalt theory) to be the characteristic rhythms of different musical forms or even speech patterns were analysed, and this analysis of sound or dance rhythms translated into visual form.

A vital part of the theoretical component of the Basic Course was the study of color theory. Indeed Itten considered this to be his major contribution to the teaching of art and sometimes designated himself 'Master of the Art of Color' when signing letters. His painting teacher at Stuttgart, Adolf Hoelzel, had extended Goethe's theory of color, which had been influential throughout Europe in the nineteenth century, having a decided effect on such Romantic artists as Turner.

Goethe's color theory was a direct rebuttal of such scientific theories as Newton's in the preceding century, and concentrated instead on the emotional and spiritual qualities of color. Hoelzel's elaboration of Goethe's theories were further extended by Itten who, three years before he began work at the Bauhaus, was to express his ideas on the inseparability of color and form; 'without color there is no form — form and color are one'. Itten further believed that the basic geometric forms of the square, the triangle and the circle are those most easily comprehended by the eye, and furthermore 'Geometric forms and the colors of the spectrum are the simplest, most sensitive forms and colors and therefore the most precise means of expression in a work of art'.

These 'means of expression' were not only to act upon the eye. Itten believed, as Goethe and artists as various as Van Gogh and Hoelzel had before him, that certain emotional states could be communicated by the use of different colors. Itten, however, in extending the theory to include not only the color but the use of basic geometric forms, was almost certainly influenced by the theory of his future colleague, Wassily Kandinsky, who published *Concerning the Spiritual in Art* in 1912. Itten's teaching that the circle signified 'uniformity, infinite, peaceful' and was blue, while the square in contrast signified 'death, dark, peace, black, red', and the triangle was white, yellow and 'vehemence', laid the ground for Kandinsky's later teaching at the Bauhaus. Such a color theory also helps explain, once the connotations are understood, the otherwise puzzling colors and forms of Peter Keler's cradle of 1922, where basic forms and primary colors are used in a literal rendering of Kandinsky's color theory. In the cradle, the 'vehement' yellow triangle is inscribed within the 'peaceful' blue circles of the rockers, and, to pursue the humorous connotation, is tempered by them, thus presumably pacifying the baby in the cradle!

The centrality of the *Vorkurs* can be seen in all aspects of the Bauhaus's development at Weimar. The emphasis on freedom of expression, combined with the disciplined elements of problem-solving and the rigorous analysis of form and color, and the stress on abstract relationships in both two and three dimensions, provided an essential springboard to the students' later development. The solid repertoire of forms and techniques introduced in the *Vorkurs* was to be drawn on and developed by the students in every workshop of the Bauhaus. This is self-evident in the early tapestries of Gunta Stölzl, for example, which are closely related to her *Vorkurs* studies. Perhaps less evident is the influence of the Basic Course on the geo-

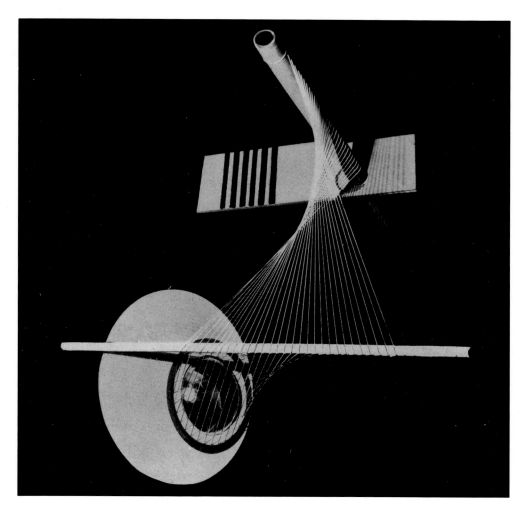

metrical forms and abstract relationships of the early work from the metal workshop at Weimar. The remarkable versatility of so many Bauhaus graduates, of which Joost Schmidt's work in several fields as designer and teacher at both the Weimar and Dessau Bauhaus is but one example, can also be seen to spring directly from the training of the Basic Course.

Above Joost Schmidt *Parabaloid Sculpture* 1928. Bauhaus Archiv, Berlin. Schmidt was one of the early Weimar students and trained in the woodcarving workshop; his hand is evident in the woodwork for the Sommerfeld House of 1920. This study was produced when he became head of the sculpture workshop at Dessau.

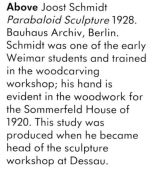

Left Gunta Stölzl, study of a thistle for Ittens' *Vorkurs*, 1920. Bauhaus Archiv, Berlin, © DACS 1991. Stölzl was one of the Bauhaus' most brilliant pupils, training and later teaching in the weaving workshop. Her early tapestries are closely related to the work she did with Itten on the preliminary course.

2

The First Masters of Form and the Sommerfeld House

The centrality of the Basic Course made Itten preeminent among the first appointments at the Bauhaus. The second most important appointment was undoubtedly that of Gerhard Marcks (1889-1981), whose work was in fact far better known at the time than Itten's. Gropius had come to know Marcks first as a fellow member of the Werkbund. Marcks had designed and executed ceramic wall decorations for the entrance hall of the model factory building designed by Gropius and Adolf Meyer for the Cologne Werkbund Exhibition of 1914. Marcks was well-known for his witty and expressive woodcuts and for his elongated and Gothic-influenced figure sculpture, both carved and cast in bronze. His work generally shows the influence both of traditional German forms and contemporary German Expressionism. Marcks had been invalided out of the war and in addition to his work as sculptor and printmaker had been teaching at the Berlin School of Arts and Crafts under the Directorship of distinguished architect Bruno Paul. Marcks' experience of working in industry, if not extensive (some of his sculptures of animals had been reproduced commercially by a porcelain manufactory), was still greater than that of any of the original Bauhaus staff with the exception of Gropius himself.

Marcks' woodcuts were later to be printed in the Bauhaus print workshop but his appointment was to the ceramic workshop as Master of Form, where he oversaw the production of some of the finest achievements of the Weimar Bauhaus. Under Marcks the pottery

workshop (which was a Bauhaus outpost at Dornburg, some 25 kilometers from Weimar – a fact that gave it a certain independence) became a highly successful realization of two aspects of the Bauhaus *Manifesto*, producing what Gropius had termed 'organic creations to be developed from craftsmanship', and also developing models for industrial production.

The third of the original Masters of Form was Lyonel Feininger (1871-1956) who was the only 'Old Master' to remain associated with the Bauhaus until it was closed down in 1933. Feininger was appointed to the printing workshop, a post to which he must have seemed particularly suited. Feininger was born in New York City of German parents who were concert musicians. At 16, a musical prodigy, he was sent to Hamburg to study, where he decided against taking up music as a career and enrolled in the School of Arts and Crafts, moving to Berlin the following year and to Paris in 1892.

When he returned to Berlin in 1893, Feininger turned to political caricatures and satirical cartoons, a career he followed for 14 years. In 1906 *The Chicago Sunday Tribune* offered him a contract which enabled him to return to Paris for two years, where he decided to give up his work for illustrated papers and become a painter. Picasso and Braque's revolutionary development of Cubism, which he saw for the first time in Paris on a brief visit in 1911, was a decisive influence on his work, transforming his former caricatural style into the disjointed architectural planes which are such a familiar feature of his later work. The architectonic nature of Feininger's work must have attracted Gropius' attention, especially perhaps the paintings which took the medieval towns and villages around Weimar (where Feininger had a studio before the war) as their subject. A marked feature of Feininger's work is the repetition of the same motif, explored in color in the medium of paint and reworked and developed in woodcut. Several of his paintings, for example, bear an obvious relationship to the key *Cathedral of the Future* image which accompanied Gropius' Bauhaus *Manifesto* of 1919. Feininger was to move with the Bauhaus to Dessau but not to teach there, although he was to occupy one of the Master's Houses until 1933 when the Bauhaus was dissolved. In 1937, when his paintings were included (together with that of all the then Bauhaus Masters) in the notorious exhibition of 'Degenerate Art' mounted by the Nazis 50 years after his departure for Europe, Feininger (who was still a US citizen) returned to live and work in New York.

Despite the caliber of his staff and the initial excitement of the enterprise, Gropius' reaction to the first display of student work in July 1919 was one of deep disappointment.

We live in dreadfully chaotic times ... and this small exhibition is their mirror image ... our impoverished State has scarcely any funds for cultural purposes any more, and is unable to take care of those who only want to occupy themselves by indulging some minor talent ... I foresee that a whole group of you will unfortunately soon be forced by necessity to take up jobs to earn money, and the only ones who will remain faithful to art will be those prepared to go hungry for it.

The aim of financial independence for the Bauhaus by means of the sale of workshop products seemed an impossibility at this stage, as so many of the students preferred the fine art dimension of the course and the re-

Below Gerhard Marcks *Die Ende* 1921, woodcut. Courtesy of the Trustees of the British Museum. Marcks came to know Gropius through his membership of the Deutscher Werkbund. He was noted for his lean elegant figure sculpture and woodcuts and contributed to Bauhaus production as a printmaker, but his appointment was to the pottery workshop as Master of Form.

Left Lyonel Feininger *Villa on the Shore* 1920, woodcut. Courtesy of the Trustees of the British Museum, © COSMOPRESS Geneva and DACS London 1991. One of the nine original Masters of Form at Weimar, Feininger was appointed to the printing workshop. He had been a cartoonist before he became a painter; his work was strongly influenced by Cubism, which transformed his caricatural style into the disjointed architectonic shapes seen here.

sources of many of the workshops were sadly limited. Contributions to Bauhaus funds were made by well-wishers and there were regular sales of works given by workshop masters.

Gropius' lack of optimism about the students' work was soon to be tempered by the success of the ceramics workshop in attracting commissions and selling work; to a lesser degree at first the textile workshop was also

Left Walter Gropius and Adolf Meyer, the Sommerfeld House, Berlin, 1921. Bauhaus Archiv, Berlin. The relatively primitive construction and exclusive use of wood seems out of keeping with Gropius' rational use of materials and insistence on simplicity, but Sommerfeld, a timber merchant, had a large amount of salvaged ship's timber available, and the design seems to reflect this marine theme.

soon to attract commissions. However the most concrete expression of Gropius' desire for a collaborative Bauhaus venture in the early years was the commission in 1920 for the Sommerfeld House, Berlin.

THE SOMMERFELD HOUSE

Gropius, in the Bauhaus *Manifesto*, had stressed that 'the ultimate aim of all creative activity is the building'. The commission for the Sommerfeld House was to provide the first opportunity for many different Bauhaus workshop masters and students (some of whom, like Joost Schmidt, later to become famous for his graphic work, had only just completed their studies on Itten's *Vorkurs*).

Adolf Sommerfeld, a friend of Gropius, was a timber merchant who, at a time when building materials were almost impossible to come by, had managed to acquire a vast amount of salvaged timber, including a quantity of teak once intended for the lining of a ship. The house for Sommerfeld (since destroyed) was built in the leafy suburb of Dahlem, which now houses West Berlin's major state museum complex. The house was one of Gropius' many private commissions at the time and Sommerfeld was prepared to allow Gropius and Meyer a completely free hand in the design. He was to prove an enlightened patron, later to sponsor the experimental Haus am Horn for the 1923 Bauhaus Exhibition as a pioneer example of public housing. Gropius saw the Sommerfeld commission as a superb opportunity to harness the skills of the Bauhaus students both in the fixtures and fittings of the building itself and the design of the interior and exterior detail. It also provided a chance for the workshop teams to collaborate on some paid work — a rare and welcome opportunity.

Right Walter Gropius and
Adolf Meyer, competition
entry for the Chicago Tribune
Tower, 1922, perspective
drawing. Bauhaus Archiv,
Berlin. This is an early
example of the Bauhaus
principles of simplicity and
use of modern industrial
materials being applied to
the high-rise style, which was
to become one of the most
recognizable features of
Modernism in architecture.

Right Karl-Peter Röhl, Bauhaus signet, 1920. This version appears on the Sommerfeld House invitation; in 1921 Röhl designed a circular version for the official seal. It is quasi-Expressionist in style, in keeping with much of the Weimar Bauhaus' work.

Below Walter Gropius and Adolf Meyer, vestibule and staircase of the Sommerfeld House, Berlin, 1921. Bauhaus Archiv, Berlin. The abstract geometric reliefs carved by Bauhaus student Joost Schmidt strike a more balanced ordered note than is conveyed by the exterior (page 37).

The salvaged ship's timbers from which the building was constructed did much to determine its form. However there is a vernacular, even folkloric, quality about the exterior which gives it the air of a primitive shelter, evoking the qualities of a large hut in the Alps or similar wild place. The 'mythic' qualities of the Sommerfeld House can also be seen to acknowledge the influence of Frank Lloyd Wright's concept of the prairie house, particularly in its log cabin appearance, with the sharply projecting roof. The mythic qualities of the house are expressed particularly clearly in the Expressionist invitation to the housewarming party in December 1920.

However it is not just the architectural form of the Sommerfeld House that is startling but the nature of its decoration which, as with the house as a whole, can now only be judged from photographs. The influence of the *Vorkurs* can be seen in the emphasis on hand craftsmanship and geometric forms and the interest in texture and surface pattern. This is particularly evident

in the carved decoration of the interior, including the carving of the inside of the front door and the metal chasing throughout. The zigzag motifs so characteristic of the carving are a dominant motif in German Expressionism, most familiar perhaps in the paintings and woodcuts of the artists of *Der Sturm* and *Die Brücke*. However it would be too simple an analysis of such a complex entity as the Haus Sommerfeld to class it solely as Expressionist. Figurative elements in Joost Schmidt's carved frieze evoking Sommerfeld's various sawmills may be read as Expressionist, or perhaps as a deliberate evocation of medieval woodcarving with its frequent symbolic references.

Another return to a traditional craft was evident in Josef Albers' stained glass windows. Both carvings and stained glass were produced in the most firmly established of the Bauhaus workshops. Although the stained glass workshop is often regarded as the Bauhaus Cinderella and did not survive the move to Dessau, it was kept busy at this time on such private commissions as the Sommerfeld House and the house built for Dr Otte in Berlin, and (also in Berlin) the staircase windows for the Ullstein Publishing Company. Josef Albers, like Joost Schmidt and Marcel Breuer, was a student at Weimar and, also like them, was to become one of the Dessau Bauhaus' famous Young Masters.

As far as can be deduced from the photographic record, Albers' glass demonstrated his early interest in

geometric form, recalling particularly his later painting series *Homage to the Square*. Indeed in its wealth of carved decoration and stained glass, together with the appliqué textile hangings made in the textile workshop to the designs of Dorte Helm (which repeated the design of the carved motifs), the Haus Sommerfeld seemed to have achieved a unity of form and decorative detail; the complete environment that was Gropius and Meyer's intention.

Marcel Breuer (1902-81), who was later to produce some of the most famous furniture designs of the Bauhaus years, received his first commissions for the Sommerfeld House. At this time Breuer was a student in the cabinetmaking workshop, which was quite distinct from the woodcarving workshop. The cabinetmaking workshop was a relatively new foundation, set up in 1921 with Gropius himself as Master of Form. Breuer's designs for the Sommerfeld House betray the influence of Itten's Basic Course in their emphasis on geometric form and contrasting textures, particularly evident in the red and black leather armchairs seen in photographs of the main hall of the house.

The Sommerfeld House as a whole, from architectural form to interior fittings, seems to have combined traditional craft and futuristic forms in a unique and exciting manner. It was visible proof of Gropius' intention that the Bauhaus should disseminate a new conception of artistic design, one that was reached as a result of co-operative effort. However, the fact that it was com-

Left The Sommerfeld House: interior carving by Schmidt, stained glass by Josef Albers and leather armchair by Marcel Breuer, all three Bauhaus students. Bauhaus Archiv, Berlin. The Sommerfeld House was the Weimar Bauhaus' first major co-operative effort.

missioned not from the Bauhaus but from Gropius' practice and was essentially a private rather than public project, thus seen only by a select few, coupled

Below Sommerfeld House: detailed view of Joost Schmidt's work on the front door and central heating covers. Bauhaus Archiv, Berlin.

Above Josef Albers *Homage to the Square: Open Outwards* oil on canvas, 23¾ × 23¾ inches (60.6 × 60.0 cm). Bildarchiv Preussischer Kulturbesitz, Berlin, © COSMOPRESS Geneva and DACS London 1991. This much later painting series demonstrates the same fascination with geometric form as Albers' student work on the stained glass for the Sommerfeld House.

with the use through force of circumstance of wood rather than industrial materials, lessened its impact. It is also an indication of the continuing lack of sympathy for the Bauhaus in Weimar that the Sommerfeld House, together with the other two projects of this period, should have been commissioned for sites in Berlin rather than the capital of the new Weimar Republic.

Nonetheless the house was a powerful demonstration of the fact that Gropius encouraged the free expression of creativity by his students, however eclectic that might be. The Sommerfeld House appears to have drawn on a heady mix of influences, from the Cubist elements in Breuer's chairs to the mix of *Sturm* and futuristic motifs of other elements of the interior. It is in one important negative aspect, however, that the Sommerfeld House may perhaps be seen as quintessentially of the Bauhaus' Weimar years. The absence of any element of industrial design is marked — even such elements as lamps and door handles were in large part made entirely by hand in the Bauhaus workshops. Thus Itten's emphasis on individual creativity and collaborative effort may be seen to have been paramount, together with the Weimar characteristic of necessity as the mother of invention. The textile workshops were not able to produce woven textiles at this time because of the shortage of materials; the appliqué wall hangings (which used small scraps of material) were an ingenious solution to the problem.

The Sommerfeld House provides the greatest possible contrast to the collaborative venture of the Dessau years, the Haus am Horn. This was a one-family house designed for the 1923 exhibition, a project financed by Sommerfeld and first mooted as a student effort to address the pressing problem of mass-housing. The prototype was produced, with the help of Gropius and Meyer's practice, by the Bauhaus workshops, which had been radically reorganized in the three years following the completion of the Sommerfeld House.

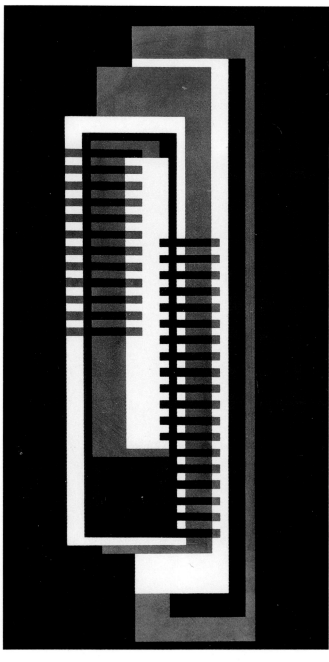

Left Josef Albers *Overlapping* 1927, sand-blasted glass panel, 23½ × 10⅞ inches (60.1 × 27.9 cm). Courtesy of the Busch-Reisinger Museum, Harvard University, © COSMOPRESS Geneva and DACS London 1991.

Left The woodworking workshop at Weimar in 1923, with work in hand on the Sommerfeld House. Bauhaus Archiv, Berlin.

The Ceramics Workshop

The ceramics workshop was the one early Bauhaus workshop to forge links with industry in its brief but highly successful life. Its achievements were among the most striking of all those of the Weimar Bauhaus, and the practices developed there provide an exemplar of Gropius' ideal of a collaborative community of artists and craftsworkers.

Gropius and Gerhard Marcks, who had been appointed Master of Form, found their early attempts to set up an experimental workshop and training ground for students in Weimar frustrated, partly because the commercial kilns available did not lend themselves to the experimental work envisaged in the Bauhaus programme. In addition, the traditionally run potteries in the town resisted the notion of an apprentice potter's training being under the tutelage of both a technical expert and a Master of Form.

Gropius and Marcks were thus forced to look elsewhere for a workplace and the fact that the pottery they eventually found was some 25 kilometers away from Weimar was to the workshop's great advantage, particularly as this distanced the day-to-day workings of students and masters from the upheavals taking place at the School in these early years. Dornburg on the Saale was difficult to reach by road or train from Weimar and living and working conditions there were primitive. There was, however, a long pottery tradition and suitable technical facilities, although the wood essential for the firing of the kilns was in short supply, as elsewhere in Germany, and what there was was fre-

quently damp – a source of constant complaint in reports back to Weimar. Part of the pottery was housed in the stables of a small but picturesque castle which had been constructed from the medieval period to the eighteenth century and was owned by the state at this time.

The scale of the original operation was very small indeed; in the earliest period the students numbered five women and two men. The pottery, when bought by the Bauhaus in 1920 (it was finally opened on October 1), was owned by Max Krehan, who necessarily became Technical Master. His collaboration with Gerhard Marcks as Master of Form came near to Gropius' ideal of such a partnership. Krehan was last in line of an old family of master potters who had supplied the needs of the local community and those of the countryside around Dornburg for generations. He was a traditional craftsman unaffected by changes in ceramic design and technology. The apprentices were taught the use of basic materials, the potter's wheel, and firing in a simple kiln. Life at Dornburg was arduous and the training rigorous. The clay had to be constantly dug out and wood chopped for the kiln. The students lived in primitive conditions, growing their own vegetables on land leased from the local community. The exacting nature of the training given may be gauged by the fact that, for the first six months of their apprenticeship, the students did nothing but throw pots during their eight-hour working day. Krehan only allowed them to experiment when they were thoroughly trained in the

Below The pottery workshop at Dornburg in about 1924. Bauhaus Archiv, Berlin. Max Krehan, appointed Craft Master by Gropius, is seated at the bench in the center, and Marguerite Friedländer, one of the workshop's most successful students, can be seen standing in the background.

basic skills. One of the apprentices, Marguerite Friedlander, already qualified as a journeyman potter, was later to recall her frustration at not being allowed to fire the pots that she and other apprentices had thrown until Krehan judged their skills at the wheel adequate. However it is evident that the atmosphere at Dornburg was conducive to the development of student creativity, and Margaret Friedlander was able to make good use of the skills taught by Krehan both in the workshop and in her later career as potter and teacher of ceramics in Holland and America.

Krehan proved the ideal craftsmaster, skilled in both technique and in his knowledge of local vernacular ceramic traditions. Krehan and Marcks formed a strong partnership, their skills complementary. In his reminiscences of the Dornburg years, Marcks stressed the workshop's emphasis on form:

The form is the main thing. It had hardly changed for centuries . . . he (Krehan) was a solid character, intelligent, too. The form had to be rediscovered first.

Marcks' own works and those produced under his tutelage from this period are distinctive in their sculptural form, recalling his own carved sculptures and the interest in medieval art shown in both his carvings and woodcuts. The pots are rustic in shape and often large in size, and their forms suggest human attributes in a manner that links them not only to the German vernacular tradition of peasant pottery but to the ancient ceramics of South America. This anthropomorphic element can be seen at its wittiest in a beaker thrown by Krehan and decorated by Marcks, which has a humorous portrait of the sculptor-potter Otto Lindig on one side and on the other a portrait of another workshop member, Johannes Dreisch. Lothar Schreyer, the stage designer and first Master of the Bauhaus Stage Workshop, writing in 1956, vividly evokes the effect of Marcks' work at the time it was produced:

We Weimar people recognized, always with astonishment, how Marcks in his plastic works succeeded in shaping

Above Marguerite Friedländer, stoneware jug with cow and ox decoration, 1922/23. Bauhaus Archiv, Berlin.

Left Henry van de Velde, coffee service designed for the Royal Saxon porcelain manufactury at Meissen, c.1905. Badisches Landesmuseum, Karlsruhe. Van de Velde's simplicity of form was particularly suited to industrial processes, as was the Bauhaus work of Otto Lindig.

Although decoration is the exception rather than the rule, the motifs are drawn from rustic themes which bear an obvious relationship to Marcks' woodcuts. The best known of these vessels is perhaps the salt-glazed bottle-shaped jug thrown by Krehan and decorated by Marcks with a humorous folkloric glazed and incised design of oxen and a ploughman. Another jug of the same period by Krehan and Marcks has a recognizably similar glazed and incised design of oxen. A jug both thrown and decorated by Margaret Friedlander, although more abstract in design, is clearly related to the former works.

It is evident that such individual hand-decorated pieces could never be adapted for production in quantity. The development of prototype vessels that could be used in serial production was a separate but linked design and technical achievement of the ceramics workshop. The pottery was fortunate in its working team: in addition to the masters, Marcks and Krehan, and experienced students like Margaret Friedlander, the workshop included Otto Lindig, who made a major contribution to the success of the pottery and helped forge its links with industrial production. Lindig was an experienced sculptor who had also trained with a porcelain manufactory. He had come to Weimar as a mature student to study at van de Velde's School of Arts and Crafts and on the outbreak of the war had transferred to the sculpture school at the School of Fine Art, graduating with his sculptor's diploma in 1917. He graduated as a journeyman potter at the age of 27 and, despite his considerable qualifications, he joined Marcks (who was only six years his senior) as an apprentice at Dornburg, realizing the unique opportunity the enterprise offered for developing his skills.

earthen vessels for the hidden postures of the human soul. Under the eyes of such a master, even the plates, pots and pitchers of the pottery became, as it were, living beings to which we had, so to speak, a personal relationship.

Krehan and Marcks' hand-thrown vessels sought to revive and reinterpret traditional vernacular forms.

Among other innovations, Lindig developed a type of convex rim for the design of his vessels. This was made possible by the development of a new type of

Left Otto Lindig, white coffee pot, 1923. Kunstsammlungen zu Weimar. Lindig was instrumental in establishing the pottery workshop's links with industrial production; this is one of several designs intended for serial production.

Below Otto Lindig, cocoa pot with mottled glaze, 1923. Kunstsammlungen zu Weimar.

earthenware at Dornburg which greatly extended the range of the workshop's production. Not content with traditional clays and firings, the team developed a close-textured earthenware fired at high temperatures which did not need to be glazed. Lindig's training as a sculptor undoubtedly contributed to his pure sense of form, which he stressed above decoration. His elegant coffee pots were later used as prototypes for industrial production in porcelain, thus bridging the gap between art and industry which was one of the original aims of the Bauhaus.

Lindig's concentration on simplicity of form was particularly suited to the industrial process and provided models for serial production, a process helped by his use of a variety of glazes rather than other forms of surface decoration. Workshop members worked from these designs to produce runs of a variety of vessels, often of different sizes, which were very popular and sold well; indeed the small workshop often had difficulty in keeping up with demand. Their first orders included a variety of specially commissioned items, from a large order to provide all the crockery for the Bauhaus canteen to an expensive hand-thrown coffee set ordered by Johannes Itten.

By 1922 Bauhaus funds were being swelled by the ceramic workshop's production, a dream of Gropius' which seemed impossible to realize at the time from other Bauhaus products. Gropius had long intended the School's future independence to be assured by the

Left Gerhard Marcks and Theodore Bogler, beaker with portrait heads of Otto Lindig (left) and Johannes Driesch. Bauhaus Archiv, Berlin.

selling of its products, but was forced in the beginning to plead for funds from wellwishers and such money-raising activities as the auctions of works by Bauhaus Masters. Within two years of being set up, the pottery workshop received several commissions, which included the production of a large order of some five hundred mugs for a hotel in Weimar. These sold at a mark apiece, and the pottery also produced simple, scaled-down mugs for use by the children of a Montes-

sori school at this period. The workshop was put under considerable strain to produce such orders and the pressure was increased by the huge success of Bauhaus ceramics at the 1923 exhibition.

Lindig's tall white coffee pot was one of several designs put into serial production at this time, apparently in the workshop itself. Its sharp rims, elegant lines and conical lid knob were much imitated in later mass-produced ceramic design throughout Europe and

Opposite Gerhard Marcks and Max Krehan, earthenware pitcher with Cubist design of fish, 1921/22. Kunstsammlungen zu Weimar. The close co-operation between Marcks as Master of Form and Krehan as Craft Master was one of the reasons for the pottery workshop's success.

Left Theodore Bogler, small tea urn in three parts, 1923. Kunstsammlungen zu Weimar. The separate elements could be made in the same molds in the workshop.

America. Lindig and Theodore Bogler appear to have worked together to develop designs which could be reproduced serially. Bogler's approach was a modular one, using the simple geometrical forms that were so central a part of the Bauhaus ethos. The separate elements of the series of teapots he designed, for example, could be made in the same molds in the workshop. The pots and the bowls that went with them thus had a family resemblance: the body of the various teapots differed only in size, while the handles could be placed at the side or be made in metal or bamboo in a style reminiscent of oriental tableware. Bogler's most ingenious modular design, which combined several of these elements, was his six-part mocha-making pot which went into production at the State Porcelain Manufactory in 1923. This clever design allowed the chocolate made in the large pot to be kept warm by means of a burner, while in its turn the coffee dripped through the tiny coffee filter at the top to achieve the requisite mix.

Right Theodore Bogler, low teapot with metal and wicker handle, 1922/23. Kunstsammlungen zu Weimar.

Less ingenious, but produced in much larger numbers and arguably the workshop's most popular design, was Bogler's set of simple kitchen storage containers of 1923. These, together with matching oil and vinegar vessels produced as models in the workshop, were for serial production by the Velten-Vordamm ceramics factory, the very first example of a collaborative craft workshop design going into mass production. The storage vessels are prominently displayed in contemporary photographs of the fitted kitchen in the experimental Haus am Horn, built for the Bauhaus Exhibition of 1923. All the Bauhaus workshops contributed to the fitting of the house, which received visitors from all over the world.

Despite such obvious achievements, however, when the Bauhaus moved to Dessau a year later the pottery was not moved with the main school, for reasons which are still unknown. The workshop team disbanded and the pottery was amalgamated into the *Bauhochschule*, the school that took over from the Bauhaus at Weimar. Of the various team members, Bogler at first worked for the stoneware pottery that had put his storage jars into production, the Velten-Vordamm ceramics manufactory, but in 1927 he relinquished his work as a potter to enter a monastery. Marguerite Friedländer and her husband Frans Wildenhaan (who had also trained at Dornburg) worked first in Holland and then in America, both teaching and producing ceramics.

Left Theodore Bogler, three-handled pitcher, 1922. Kunstsammlungen zu Weimar.

Below Theodore Bogler, kitchen storage jars, porcelain, 1922. Kunstsammlungen zu Weimar. This range was manufactured from 1923 by the Velten-Vordamm ceramics factory and can be seen in the kitchen of the Haus am Horn built for the 1923 Bauhaus Exhibition (page 88).

Left Otto Lindig, large pitcher-shaped storage jar with conical lid, 1922. Kunstsammlungen zu Weimar. The simplicity of form favored by Lindig was the Dornburg pottery's most significant legacy to subsequent potters.

Opposite Gerhard Marcks and Max Krehan, bottle-shaped pitcher c.1922, salt glaze, with oxen and ploughman decoration. Bauhaus Archiv, Berlin. The combination of Krehan's traditional craft skills and Marcks' distinctively sculptural decoration typify the earliest Dornburg work.

Marcks taught pottery elsewhere, while continuing his work as a sculptor and printmaker at the Dessau Bauhaus.

Lindig continued to teach at Dornburg, later becoming Director of the pottery. As both teacher and potter his was arguably the most influential career of all those at Dornburg, and the values of refined and elegant simplicity of form which he promulgated above those of surface decoration may be seen to have had a major influence on later twentieth-century ceramics.

Changes at Weimar

While the pottery was achieving success at Dornburg, all was not well at Weimar, where there was continued privation and internal dissension, much of it centered around Itten and his influence. Gropius continued to make distinguished appointments, however, primarily of painters, including Paul Klee (1879-1940), who joined the teaching team in 1920, and Wassily Kandinsky (1866-1944), who became a Master in 1922. Kandinsky, a Russian who had studied in Munich and was forced to leave Germany at the beginning of the war, was regarded as the most significant abstract painter of the time. He had also played a leading role in the reform of art education in the newly developing Soviet Union, becoming Professor of Painting at the State Art Workshops, Moscow, in 1918 and founding the Russian Academy of Artistic Sciences in 1921. In these ventures he was influenced by Gropius' ideas and the two maintained a correspondence on educational matters until Kandinsky came to teach at Weimar.

Kandinsky returned to Germany in 1921, disillusioned by current events and the position regarding progressive educational reform in Russia. His fame preceded him to Weimar; his *Concerning the Spiritual in Art* of 1912 was one of the most influential works of artistic theory of its time, in which Kandinsky employed his formidable knowledge of philosophy, psychology and science. All Bauhaus students would have been introduced to his ideas on the Basic Course. As a painter, Kandinsky is generally credited with the first entirely

non-figurative painting, a watercolor, as early as 1910. Kandinsky believed that 'painting can develop the same energies as music'. His series of *Improvisations*, for example, were spontaneous abstract expressions of particular feelings, intended to have an effect on the beholder similar to that of music on the listener. He was to contribute two vital components to the Basic Course: analytical drawing and the theoretical analysis of color and form. Kandinsky was 56 when he came to the Bauhaus in 1922, an austere figure of whom his students were much in awe.

Paul Klee, 13 years younger than Kandinsky and no less famous today as one of the leading painters of the twentieth century, joined the teaching team in 1920. Klee's work was fantastical, witty and dreamlike. Experienced as a graphic artist, he had reached maturity as a painter relatively late and in 1920 his work was only just beginning to receive international recognition. Klee's appointment caused some consternation among his new colleagues, particularly as he had no former experience of teaching; Schlemmer recalled that Klee's work 'appears to inspire the greatest shaking of heads, as a kind of "art for art's sake" removed from every practical purpose'. Klee was already thinking along the same lines as Gropius, however, and had long perceived what he termed individualistic art as a 'capitalist luxury' and foresaw that: 'a new kind of art could enter the crafts and produce great results. For there would no longer be academies, only art schools for craftsmen.' In this as with other appointments, Gropius knew his man; Klee approached his new teaching role with intuitive flair and from an extraordinary depth of knowledge, and was extremely popular with his students.

Klee, who was Swiss, and a virtuoso violinist at the age of 12, trained in Munich and was a member of *Der Blaue Reiter*, a loosely organized group of Expressionist painters, from 1911 (where he first met Kandinsky). He was widely traveled and a trip to North Africa in 1914 was a decisive factor in his development. The cuboid shapes of the buildings and the bright colors of the landscape were a revelation; 'color has taken possession of me . . . color and I are one'. At the Bauhaus Klee's new experience of teaching persuaded him to analyze his own creative processes in order to convey information to others. His teaching responsibilities were considerable; after Itten's departure he was appointed Master of the stained glass workshop, directed courses in weaving and painting, and shared the teaching of Basic Design with Kandinsky. His *Pedagogic Sketchbooks*, published as the second of the Bauhaus Books in 1925, help explain his theories and teaching processes. Klee's complex theories, though no less subtle than Kandinsky's, were decidedly less dogmatic in formulation and expression. Klee allowed the students space for their own explorations while developing a system which attempted to explain the relationships between colors, lines (Klee's is the famous definition of drawing as 'taking a line for a walk') and even entire compositions.

Both Klee and Kandinsky made their major contribution to Bauhaus teaching in the field of Basic Design. Like their respective paintings, their lectures were entirely different from each other's. Although both artists aimed to ground their teaching in analysis of the creative process, Klee believed that the artist must 'place himself at the starting point in creation', and in

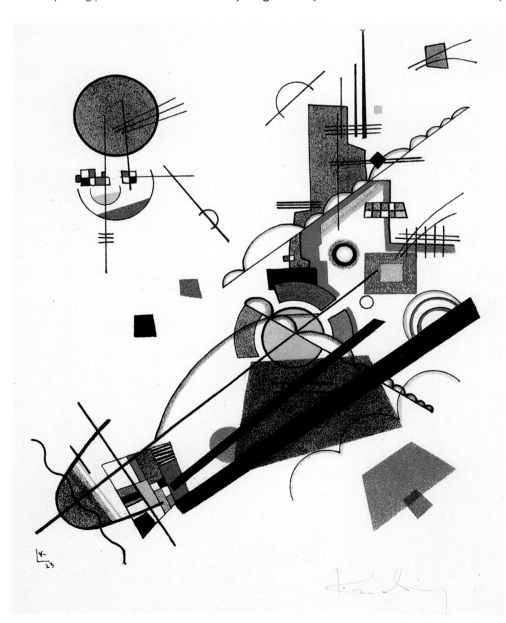

his 1924 lecture 'On Modern Art', he compared the creative process to the growth of the trunk of a tree:

The artist stands as the trunk of the tree, he does nothing other than gather and pass on what comes to him from the depths. He neither serves nor rules – he transmits. His position is humble and the beauty at the crown is not his own. He is merely a channel.

This organic approach may be contrasted to Kandinsky's in *Point and Line to Plane*, published as a Bauhaus Book in 1926. Kandinsky believed that:

The progress achieved by systematic research will give birth to a dictionary of elements, a 'grammar' and finally to a theory of composition that will overrule the boundaries of the individual arts and refer to art in general.

The Bauhaus students were uniquely fortunate in their tutors. The wealth of skill and experience offered by Gropius' choice of Masters, and the extraordinary quality of the teaching programme, does much to explain the quality of the artefacts produced in the Bauhaus workshops in the years following the crises of the early 1920s.

A less famous figure than either Klee or Kandinsky, but no less important to the future development of the Bauhaus, was the painter Georg Muche, 1895-1987, appointed at the early age of 25 in 1921. Muche, an Expressionist painter who had exhibited with *Der Sturm* in Berlin and had also taught at the Sturm school, shared some of Itten's mystical beliefs, but was clear about the situation as he saw it on his arrival at the Bauhaus and his intentions concerning his work there. He wrote:

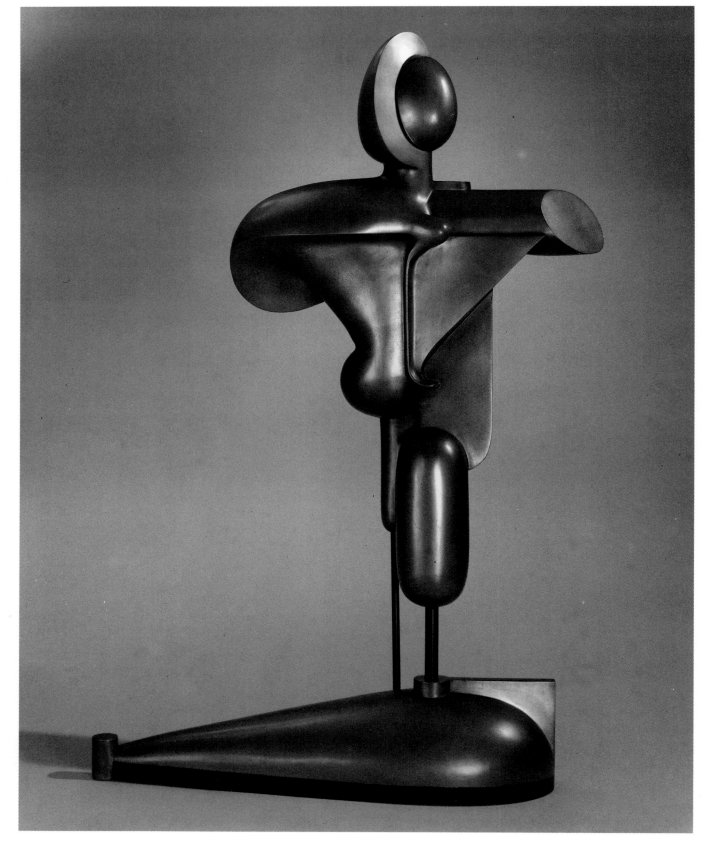

Right Oskar Schlemmer *Abstract Figure* original 1921, cast 1962, bronze with matted nickel, 41½ × 24⅝ × 8½ inches (105.4 × 62.6 × 21.6 cm). The Baltimore Museum of Art, Alan and Janet Wurtzburger Collection, BMA 1966.55.28, © The Oskar Schlemmer Family Estate. Schlemmer, who originally came to Weimar to discuss publication of some of his graphics in the Bauhaus yearbook *Utopia*, was initially appointed Master of Form in the sculpture workshop.

Left Friedl Dicker, programme design for a Bauhaus evening with the poet Else Lasker Schuler. Bauhaus Archiv, Berlin. Parties and social gatherings formed an important and unifying feature of life in the early years at Weimar. The Expressionist style of the programme reflects the artistic mood of the youthful Bauhaus.

The art of handwork was not my thing. The ideas of Ruskin, Morris and German Werkbund were not for me . . . I wanted to remain a painter and not become involved in polemics about the social significance of art.

When appointed Master of Form in the weaving workshop he vowed:

I promised myself never in my life to weave a thread, tie a knot, or make a textile design with my own hand. I have kept that promise.

Elsewhere he wrote that he had come to Weimar 'not because of the programme but because of the people'. In spite his comparative youth, Muche was given the enormous responsibility of taking over the entire teaching of Itten's Basic Course while Itten took a sabbatical period at the Madaznan center at Herrliberg.

Despite his initial reservations, Muche was to change his conceptions (and indeed his painting style) radically during the six years he spent at the Bauhaus in both Weimar and Dessau. He was to remain as Form Master in the weaving workshop for the entire period, and demonstrated that extraordinary versatility that is so marked a feature of the careers of both staff and students at the Bauhaus. While continuing to teach, paint and make prints, he provided architectural designs for the experimental Haus am Horn for the 1923 exhibition.

The painter and theater designer Oskar Schlemmer (1888-1943), whose work in the theater workshop was soon to contribute to the fame of the revitalized Bauhaus, also became a Master in this period. Like Itten, Schlemmer had trained under the painter and theorist Adolf Hoelzel at Stuttgart. Gropius first saw his mural paintings at the Cologne Werkbund Exhibition, and Schlemmer originally came to the Bauhaus with the intention of discussing the inclusion of some of his graphic work in the limited collectors' annual publication *Utopia*, which was co-edited by Itten and printed at the Bauhaus. In 1920 the Bauhaus was in a difficult

Above Paul Klee *Three Houses* 1922, watercolor on laid paper bordered by violet watercolor mounted on light cardboard, 7⅞ × 11⅞ inches (20 × 30.2 cm). Metropolitan Museum, New York, Berggreuen Klee collection. Klee joined the Weimar Bauhaus in 1920, initially as Master of Form in the bookbinding workshop.

Right Wassily Kandinsky, Bauhaus postcard 3, 1923. Bauhaus Archiv, Berlin, © ADAGP Paris and DACS London 1991. One of a series of postcards produced to publicize the 1923 Bauhaus Exhibition.

situation, so difficult indeed that Schlemmer, whose lively reminiscences provide an invaluable insight into these years, was at first reluctant to take up his appoint-ment, and even when appointed did not live at Weimar for some time, as he continued to work at the theater in Stuttgart. Schlemmer was trenchant in his initial criticisms of the situation as he found it at Weimar: 'They want to do much, but can do nothing for lack of funds. So they play about.' In February 1921 he wrote . . .

The Bauhaus programme has attracted a fearless band of young people . . . All this means that the Bauhaus is building something quite different from what was planned. He (Gropius) wants an artist to have character, and this should come first and not later. Yet at times he appears alarmed at the outcome, no work gets done, but there is a great, great deal of talk.

Gropius was indeed aware of what Schlemmer described as the student's expression of their 'inner confusion' by 'throwing aside conventions and inhibitions and sliding into the Great Indolence'. The Director's significant comments on the first exhibition of students' work has already been noted, and in January 1921 he published the formalized pedagogical programme and school statutes, *The Statutes of the State-run Bauhaus in Weimar*. Particularly interesting are the rules governing examination, both at the end of the compulsory six-month Basic Course and at the end of the three-year workshop training programme.

At the end of the legally set duration of their apprenticeship and after fulfilment of the legal requirements, apprentices may enrol for their journeyman's examination . . . the examinations are taken before the Appointments Board.

Far left Georg Muche *Abstract Composition* 1916. Courtesy of Barry Friedmann Ltd. Muche, an Expressionist painter who had exhibited with *Der Sturm*, developed unusually from abstraction to figuration.

Left Paul Klee, Bauhaus postcard 4, 1923. Bauhaus Archiv, Berlin. Both Masters and students contributed to the postcard series produced to publicize the 1923 Exhibition.

The Bauhaus concept of a diagnostic Basic Course or foundation course followed by three years of specialist training has since provided the model for the training of artists and crafts-students throughout the world.

The Bauhaus was at all times during its comparatively brief existence difficult to enter, and indeed to stay within after the compulsory six-month Basic Course. At any one time there were only some 100 students and the entire register of Bauhaus trained *Bauhaüsler* is only 1,250. The hurdles presented to the intending student can be gauged by the admission forms for the *Vorkurs*. One student, Luise Molzahn, was interviewed by Gropius, Itten, Feininger, Muche and Schlemmer in April 1921, but when the Basic Course was completed six months later she failed the examination that would have allowed her to proceed to a training in the weaving workshop. This was by no means an unusual occurrence; the difficulties of completing the courses added to the *Bauhaüsler* sense of privilege at being part of such an exclusive group despite, and in some measure because of, the privations of the early years. At the beginning times were so hard that Bauhaus students, many of whom had served in the war, were distinctive in and around Weimar by reason of their appearance alone. Clothing was so hard to come by in the years immediately following the war that many of them wore converted army uniforms, brightly dyed and ingeniously remade into what was almost to become a Bauhaus uniform. Most students were dependent on the Bauhaus canteen for their food and it became a central focus for both students and staff. When commissions were available, Gropius arranged a system of payment for the workshop students involved, thus providing them with essential funds as well as preparing them for professional life.

The sense of being part of a disparate yet united international group working in a common cause was enhanced by the famous parties and celebrations that were to form such an important part of life in the early years at Weimar. Felix Klee, who was accepted as the youngest student (at 14) in fall 1921, after his father Paul

began to teach at Weimar, vividly evokes the costume balls, each on a different theme, and the four seasonal festivals. There was the Festival of Lanterns to celebrate Gropius' birthday; Midsummer Night; the Dragon Festival in October where 'we went up to one

Below Herbert Bayer, poster for Wassily Kandinsky's sixtieth birthday exhibition in Dessau, 1926. Bauhaus Archiv, Berlin, © DACS 1991.

Right Oskar Schlemmer, drawings for Schlemmer's course on 'Man', taught at Dessau 1928/29. © The Oskar Schlemmer Family Estate.

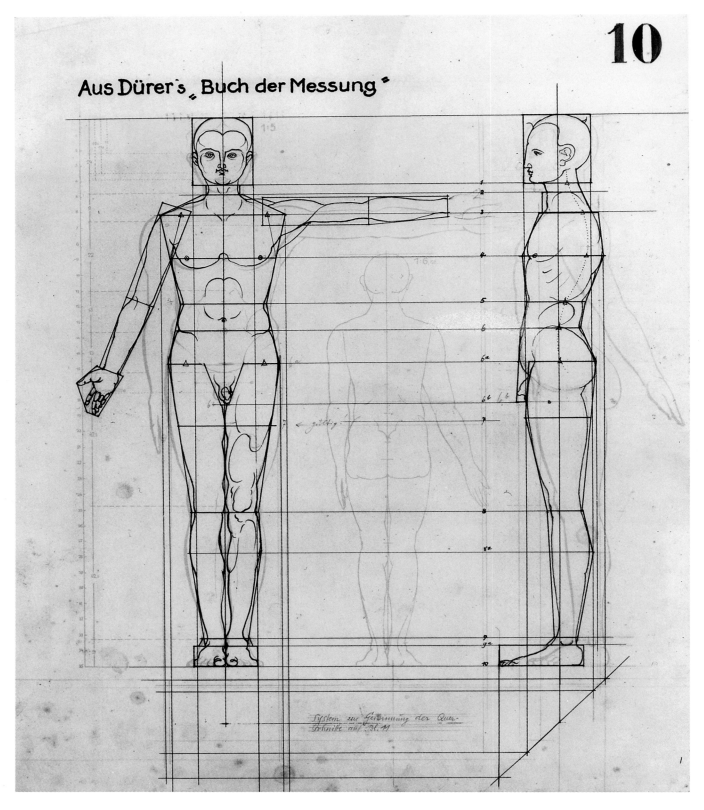

10

Aus Dürer's „Buch der Messung"

Right Oskar Schlemmer, seal of the State Bauhaus, 1922, lithograph. © The Oskar Schlemmer Family Estate. The original seal designed by Karl-Peter Röhl was replaced at Gropius' instigation by Schlemmer's more formal image, with its economical lines and obvious debt to De Stijl.

Opposite László Moholy-Nagy, *Funkturm, Berlin*, c.1925, photograph. Bauhaus Archiv, Berlin. This dramatic view looking down from the top of the Berlin Radio Tower is typical of Moholy-Nagy's imaginative work with a camera.

of the neighboring small hills ... to let our abstract dragons sail in the wind, much to the surprise of the inhabitants below'. Another student, Liz Abegs, described the first Bauhaus Christmas in 1919:

Christmas was indescribably beautiful, something quite new, a 'Festival of Love' in every particular ... beneath the tree everything white, on it countless presents. Gropius read the Christmas story. Emmy Hein sang. Gropius gave us all presents ... then a big meal ... Gropius served each person in turn. Like the washing of the feet.

By the early 1920s, however, Gropius was hard-pressed on all fronts. He had to fight to obtain state funds and withstand attacks from local opposition forces, from Nationalists to those opposed to the Bauhaus by reason of its association with the former Academy of Fine Art and the School of Arts and Crafts at Weimar. In April 1921 opponents of the Bauhaus and its methods succeeded in obtaining the dissolution of

the union between these two institutions which, two years before, had formed the Bauhaus. The reconstituted Academy of Fine Art was reopened in the same building as the Bauhaus and three of the newly appointed Bauhaus teachers who had originally worked for the Academy returned to working there, followed by several students who disagreed with Bauhaus principles. Student and staff opposition had been simmering for some time, much of it directed against Gropius or Itten in what was now perceived as an opposition of ideology between them. This apparent 'schism' exacerbated the Director's problems but also forced him to reconsider the aims of the Bauhaus and the direction it was to take.

An important signifier of Gropius' thinking at this time was his decision to have the Bauhaus seal redesigned. The original design by Karl Peter Röhl was decidedly Expressionist in its symbolism and lettering, showing man the builder supporting the ultimate artefact, the building. The new design by Schlemmer, completed in fall 1921, was elegant and decidedly minimalist, depicting man at the center of the universe. The design demonstrated the considerable influence of the avant-garde international movement De Stijl, centered in Holland, which had already had a major influence on architecture and design throughout Europe and was soon to have an important impact on other forms of activity at the Bauhaus.

Theodore van Doesburg, architect, artist and founding father of De Stijl, had come to Weimar in the spring of 1921 to set up a De Stijl course, which consisted of a series of public lectures and also offered free tuition in composition to Bauhaus students. This attracted a considerable number of disaffected *Bauhäusler*, including

Below Theodore van Doesburg *Countercomposition V* 1924, oil on canvas, 39 × 39 inches (100 × 100 cm). Stedelijk Museum, Amsterdam.

Above László Moholy-Nagy *A II* 1924, oil on canvas, 45⅝ × 53⅝ inches (115.9 × 136.3 cm). The Solomon R Guggenheim Museum, New York. Gropius chose Moholy as successor to the inspirational Johannes Itten, rather than van Doesburg.

the designer of the original Bauhaus signet, Karl Peter Röhl. The publication of the magazine *De Stijl* was also moved to Weimar and, while van Doesburg made no secret of his admiration for Gropius' achievement at the Bauhaus, he was equally clear in his public utterances as to how much he and his fellow De Stijl members (who had originally included such influential figures as the architect and designer Gerrit Rietveld and the painter Piet Mondrian) deplored the direction Bauhaus teaching had taken. The September 1922 edition of *De Stijl* contained a van Doesburg-inspired out-and-out attack on what was seen as the Bauhaus' lack of productivity:

Where is there any attempt to unify several disciplines, at the unified combination of space, form and color? Pictures, nothing but pictures ... graphics and individual pieces of sculpture ... In order to reach the goals aimed for by the Bauhaus in its manifesto other masters are required, masters who know what the creation of a unified work of art entails and can demonstrate their ability to create such a work ...

Van Doesburg's presence in Weimar was a confrontational move made apparently to force Gropius (who much respected De Stijl) into appointing him to the Bauhaus staff. Most of the other members of the original De Stijl had moved on and van Doesburg felt the need of a new arena for his ideas in which to enhance a growing international reputation. Indeed Gropius had already suggested van Doesburg's name for inclusion among the teaching staff, a move welcomed in a shrewd comment by Feininger, 'because he would represent the opposite pole to much of the exaggerated Romanticism which haunts us here'. However Feininger could also see that van Doesburg in time 'would probably ... like Itten ... want to take over everything'. Van Doesburg, in what might be perceived as another publicly provocative move, organized the Constructivist and Dadaist Congress in Weimar in 1922. This brought to Weimar such leading Russian Constructivists as El Lissitsky, the Hungarian László Moholy-Nagy and the Dadaist Tristan Tzara. The presence of such influential artists in Weimar — not to speak of the 'happenings' organized by van Doesburg as part of the Congress programme in which his wife Nelly played her own disharmonic compositions and van Doesburg and others harangued the audience to such effect that Bauhaus students defected — were to help concentrate Gropius' mind.

It was as though the use of 'romantic' as a term of abuse directed at Bauhaus students by their former peers who had defected to the van Doesburg camp found its mark with their Director. The utopian socialism and romantic medievalism of the Bauhaus *Manifesto* had always seemed ill-at-ease with the radical Modernism of its architect's Fagus factory. Now Gropius' ideals of the Fagus factory resurfaced. It was as though a project such as the Sommerfeld villa, hand-crafted with no reference to industrial design, had been an aberration.

In February 1922 Gropius circulated a memorandum among the Masters of Form which is the key to understanding the decisive changes he was about to make at this pivotal point in the life of the Bauhaus. He begins:

Master Itten recently demanded that one must decide *either* to produce work as an individual in complete opposition to the economic world outside *or* to search for an understanding with industry . . . I look for unity in *the combination* not the division of these forms of life.

Gropius goes on to confirm his faith in modernity and the industrial age.

Whenever the question is raised about which forms created by recent generations may later be seen to be characteristic of our times, the work of the architects, academicians and artist-craftsmen disappears from view. On the other hand . . . the world of forms which emerged from and in company with the machine asserts itself: the new means of travel (steam-engine, aeroplane), factories, American silos and things which we use daily that were produced by machines.

To put this into context, it is as well to remember that Gropius' ideas were part and parcel of the new feeling in Germany at this time, a feeling that rejected Expressionism and in all forms of cultural activity generally sought *neue Sachlichkeit*, loosely translatable as 'a new directness of approach, a new objectivity, a new sobriety'. Certainly the polarities represented by van Doesburg's call to reason and the extreme mysticism of Itten's individualistic crafts-based approach in the latter years of his teaching seem to have presented Gropius with the space in which to hold a position on the middle ground, and from there to achieve a synthesis of art and technology.

The call to order represented by Gropius' memorandum to the Masters of Form had but one inevitable conclusion; the removal of Itten from his position of power on the *Vorkurs* and in the workshops. The man whom Gropius had termed *le clou* (nail, that which holds things together) of the Bauhaus was persuaded, in a series of complex diplomatic moves on Gropius' part, to resign. Itten gave up the teaching of the *Vorkurs* in the fall of 1922 and finally left the following spring to pursue his studies at the Mazdaznan center at Herrliberg until 1926, then to establish his own art school in Berlin. He was to spend the rest of his life, until his death in Zurich in 1967, in the teaching of art and design.

Van Doesburg was never offered a teaching position at the Bauhaus. Gropius instead made an enlightened and indeed exciting choice as Itten's successor. László Moholy-Nagy (1895-1946) was the direct antithesis of Itten in every possible way and his distinctive qualities added to the uniquely strong teaching team which now included Paul Klee and Wassily Kandinsky as well as Schlemmer and Muche. Moholy-Nagy was Hungarian, a self-taught innovative artist of extraordinary versatility. He believed that it was of the utmost importance for an artist to work in many media: he was a radical designer and typographer; he produced various forms of three-dimensional constructions and collages; and some of the most distinctive photographs of the period. He considered a knowledge of photography vital to any one who wished to be considered visually literate, and his own radical photographs and experiments in photography included a revival of one of the earliest forms of photography, first used in 1839; exposing objects on light-sensitive paper (without the use of a camera) to form abstract 'photograms'. In his essay of 1922 *Constructivism and the Proletariat*, Moholy proclaimed the centrality of the machine:

The reality of our century is technology; the invention, construction and maintenance of machines. To be a user of machines is to be of the spirit of this century. It has replaced the transcendental spiritualism of past eras.

Moholy's very appearance signified his belief in both modern technology and the 'new objectivity'. His customary dress was a kind of industrial boilersuit, worn with shirt and tie and round spectacles with nickel frames — the very antithesis of the 'transcendental spiritualism' of Itten's monastic robe and shaven head. In Moholy's essay of 1922, the year before he took over the teaching of the *Vorkurs*, the extent of the difference between his and Itten's ideology can be grasped by such passages as the following:

Everyone is equal before the machine. I can use it, so can you. It can crush me, the same can happen to you. There is no tradition in technology, no class-consciousness. Everyone can be the machine's master or its slave.

Moholy had arrived in Germany only a year before, and his German was always heavily accented and never fluent; the students' affectionate puns on his name included 'Holy Mahogany'. He had worked his way across Germany as a sign painter and was noted for his enthusiasm as well as his extraordinary natural gift for teaching. Paul Citroen, who was at one time one of Itten's most devoted followers, evokes an image of Moholy as 'bursting into the Bauhaus circle like a strong, eager dog . . . sniffing out with unfailing scent the still unsolved tradition-bound problems in order to attack them'. With the key figures now in place, the history of the Bauhaus was set to move into an entirely new phase.

Opposite László Moholy-Nagy at the Bauhaus in 1925. Bauhaus Archiv, Berlin, photograph courtesy of Lucia Moholy. Moholy is pictured in his customary boilersuit, a pointed contrast to Itten's studied spirituality.

'Art & Technology: A New Unity'

Left Naum Slutzky, copper casket, 1920. Bauhaus Archiv, Berlin. Slutzky was the first Craft Master in the metal-working workshop; his work typifies the clearly Expressionist and symbolic nature of much early Bauhaus metalwork.

The change of emphasis at the Bauhaus reflected in the departure of Itten and the appointment of Moholy-Nagy in 1923 can perhaps be most starkly seen in a radical change of approach not only to the means of production but to the use of materials. Whereas Itten's teaching was subjective in its approach, that of Moholy was decidedly objective. A study of the objects produced in the metal workshops between 1919 and 1925 makes this clear.

According to the original Bauhaus programme, the purpose of the metal-working workshop was to train 'blacksmiths, locksmiths, founders, metal-turners, enamellers and chasers'. The young Viennese jeweller Naum Slutzky was the first Craft Master, succeeded by Christian Dell in 1922. Itten was Form Master throughout this period and the influence of his teaching is particularly strong, especially given that in many ways the students would have regarded the specialist workshop training as a reinforcement and extension of Itten's ideas on the Basic Course.

The origins of the metal workshop under the direction of Slutzky lay in techniques associated with jewelry making, work which included jewelry of a quasi-ritualistic design and vessels of a symbolic nature which appear decidedly Expressionistic. Such objects were later classified by one student as 'spiritual samovars and intellectual doorknobs' (a reference to the metal door fittings made by the workshop for the Sommerfeld House).

Characteristic of this mode is the spherical copper casket made by Slutzky in 1920. This object of indeterminate function is hand-tooled in a repeating pattern of hammered arcs, recalling the *Vorkurs'* emphasis on the exploration of contrasting textures and symbolic shapes. Indeed the shape can be seen as mystical; it is a perfect sphere, divided into hemispheres at the point approximating to the golden mean. The shape and decoration recalls medieval church plate. A student work produced under the same influences is Gyula Pap's seven-branched candlestick of 1923, which also

Right Gyula Pap, seven-branched candlestick, 1923. Bauhaus Archiv, Berlin, © DACS 1991. An example of the hand-crafted, decorative work produced under Itten, as Master of Form.

Left Josef Hoffmann, silver fruit basket, 1904. Courtesy of the Trustees of the Victoria and Albert Museum, London. Hoffmann's work for the Wiener Werkstätte is typified by the angular forms of this piece. The ideas and products of the Wiener Werkstätte were particularly influential in the Bauhaus metal workshops.

Below Marianne Brandt, tea infuser and cream jug, 1924, bronze, ebony handles, silver mounts. Kunstsammlungen zu Weimar. These early pieces show the influence of Itten's *Vorkurs* in their emphasis on basic geometric shapes.

has a ritualistic, hand-crafted appearance. Objects such as these, produced under the tutelage of Itten and Slutzky, were clearly intended as decorative works, *objets de vertu*. The materials used were indicative of their purpose. Bronze, silver and copper are all traditional metal-working materials suitable for the production of unique hand-crafted designs, not for machine production. Because materials were scarce, so-called German silver, an alloy of 50% copper, 25% zinc and 25% nickel, was used, as was tombac, an alloy of copper and zinc.

In 1922 Christian Dell, a silversmith who had worked with van de Velde, was appointed Craft Master. Dell had worked in the elegant geometric tradition of the Viennese Workshops (Wiener Werkstätte), influenced by the silver designs of such craftsmen as Josef Hoff-

mann (1870-1956) and continuing the traditional craft approach to working in precious or semi-precious metals. The influence of the English designer Christopher Dresser (1834-1904) may also be seen in the work of this period, especially with regard to the use of simple geometric forms and minimal decoration.

Bauhaus metalwork of this period was frequently concerned with the paraphernalia of tea and coffee making. Tea infusers (sometimes in sets), tea pots, tea caddies and tea sets, coffee pots and coffee services all provided opportunities to experiment with design and methods of production. The students were encouraged to apply the principles of the Basic Course to the handcrafting of such objects. Marianne Brandt (1893-1983) had studied painting and sculpture in Weimar in 1911, returning in 1924 to the Bauhaus,

Above Marianne Brandt, tea and coffee service, 1924. Bauhaus Archiv, Berlin.

Left Christopher Dresser, egg steamer (c.1884) and claret jug (1879), brass and glass. Courtesy of the Trustees of the Victoria and Albert Museum, London. The work of English designer Christopher Dresser, distinguished by its use of simple geometric forms and minimal decoration, influenced metalwork at the Bauhaus more than a generation later.

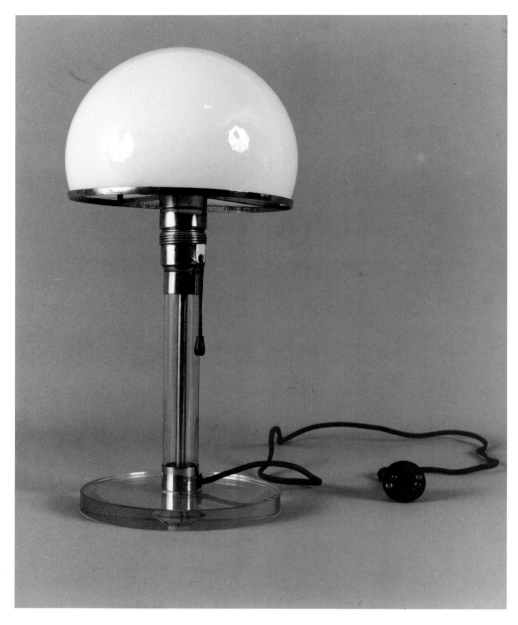

designs which have become cult-objects of the Weimar Bauhaus. She described her initial reception as the only woman in the metal workshop:

At first I was not accepted with pleasure . . . there was no place for a woman in a metal workshop . . . they expressed their displeasure by giving me all sorts of dull and dreary work. How many little hemispheres did I most patiently hammer out of brittle new silver, thinking that was the way it had to be and all beginnings had to be hard. Later things settled down and we got on well together.

So well indeed that in 1928 she became temporary head of the workshop. Brandt writes of the near-obsessive workshop ethos of 'wanting to return to the simplest forms', and certainly basic geometric forms are constant motifs in the designs of the period, recalling the Basic Course's emphasis on the importance of the circle, triangle, square, sphere, pyramid and cube.

Functionality was also of prime importance — how the spout of a teapot poured, how the handle balanced, how the lid fitted, was of no less importance than the geometric form. Nonetheless the seemingly endless stream of objects associated with tea and coffee making, however functional their appearance, were still laboriously produced entirely by hand.

Moholy's arrival in 1923 radically altered workshop production, particularly with regard to lighting, which was to become one of the major success stories of the Bauhaus, and in time provided an essential source of income. At Weimar Moholy encouraged the use of modern metals in conjunction with glass, which produced objects in which no trace of the *facture* (method by which it was made) can be seen. This objective approach, in which the 'maker's mark' is obliterated,

Above William Wagenfeld and Karl Jucker, table lamp, 1924. Bauhaus Archiv, Berlin. The elegant functionality of this lamp, one of the best-known objects of Bauhaus design, belies the labor-intensive method of production.

Right Marianne Brandt, tea plate, 1923/24. Kunstsammlungen zu Weimar. The clean simple lines echo the elegant geometric tradition of Hoffmann and Dresser.

Below Marianne Brandt, bedside light, 1928. Courtesy of Barry Friedmann Ltd. Another Bauhaus classic, which was manufactured by Korting and Matthiessen (Kandem) from 1928.

Right Marianne Brandt and Hans Przyrembel, adjustable aluminum ceiling light, 1926. Bauhaus Archiv, Berlin. This design was manufactured and was used in the Bauhaus workshops.

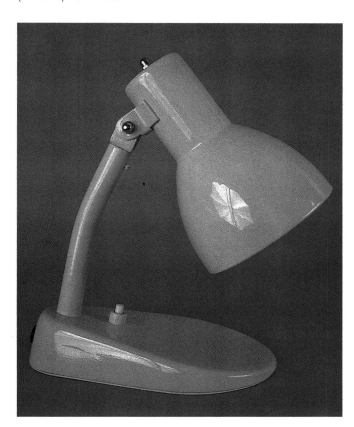

represents a fundamental break with the past and was not confined to the work of the metal workshop. Of equal importance is Moholy's emphasis on a collaborative rather than an individual approach to design. The design of each project was subject to group discussion from the very beginning and this, together with close collaboration with such lighting-manufacturers as Kandem and Osram in order to discuss design priorities, does much to explain the success of the Bauhaus lighting design.

The well-known tablelamp designed by Wilhelm Wagenfeld and Karl Jucker may be taken as a case in point to illustrate this new approach. The working parts of the lamp, including the flex, are all visible and the opaque glass shade, of a type used formerly only for industrial lighting, diffuses the light. The simple geometric shapes of the component parts are obviously related to Bauhaus teaching, and the whole design has an elegant functionality which was innovative at the time and still continues to be influential. Despite the industrial appearance of the lamp, it is ironic that the various components were all laboriously assembled by hand in the Bauhaus workshop. Wagenfeld, who became one of Germany's leading designers for industry, known not only for his lighting designs but for the radical modular glassware 'Kubus', was later to write that the design of the lamp was influenced by Moholy's paintings and that the Bauhaus team was convinced that the design could be successfully marketed. However the labor-intensive production method made the lamps prohibitively expensive; 'retailers and manufacturers laughed at our efforts ... (the lamp was) a crippled, bloodless picture in glass and metal'.

Right Wilhelm Wagenfeld, coffee and tea service, c.1924, German silver and brass with ebony handles. Kunstsammlungen zu Weimar.

Below Logo for Kandem, trade name of lighting manufacturers Korting and Matthiessen. Bauhaus Archiv, Berlin. The logo was designed by Herbert Schurman in 1932 and was the winning entry in a Bauhaus competition. The working relationship between the Bauhaus and Kandem, which began in 1928, was one of the most successful of the School's partnerships with industry.

Other lighting projects were successfully translated into machine production, however, and it may safely be said that the Bauhaus designs proved a watershed in twentieth-century lighting design, both domestic and public. Simple and elegant domestic fixtures which translated the opaque glass hemispheres previously used only in industrial lighting systems, and the use of chrome and aluminium in conjunction with frosted or milk glass, were contributing factors to the success of the Bauhaus designs, which radically re-addressed the problems of light's intensity and reflection.

The system of workshop collaboration established at Weimar by Moholy and his team continued at Dessau. Marianne Brandt produced designs in collaboration with several colleagues, including Hans Przyrembel. The aluminum counterweighted adjustable ceiling light manufactured by Schwintzer & Gräff, Berlin (who were to manufacture many Bauhaus designs) became a standard fixture in the Bauhaus workshops, and when color-sprayed was also suitable for domestic use.

Another of Brandt's collaborations, with Hein Briedendieck, produced what was to become the definitive twentieth-century desk or bedside lamp, with an adjustable shade and push-button switch located in its solidly weighted base. Some of the ceiling-mounted designs by Max Krajewski were used throughout the new Bauhaus building at Dessau. These used simple hemispherical shapes of milk glass either to produce background lighting or, with the addition of a simple system of reflective dishes, to provide directional light for working purposes. The use of such in-house designs in the Bauhaus buildings themselves was of utmost importance, as the School buildings and

Above Wolfgang Tümpel, teapot and tea-set, c.1924, silver, gold, and chrysophase. Kunstgewerbe Sammlung der Stadt Bielefeld.

Left Otto Rittweger and Wolfgang Tümpel, tea infusers and stand, c.1924, German silver. Germanisches Nationalmuseum Nürnberg. The infusers can be seen, together with other products of the metal workshop, in the photograph of Walter and Ise Gropius at Dessau (page 98).

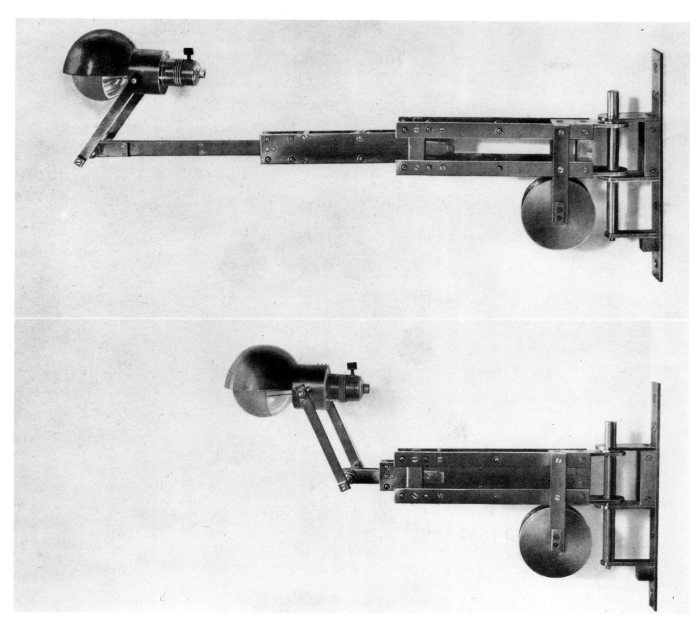

Gropius' Director's House quickly became a mecca for visitors from all over the world.

Extendable wall-mounted lighting prototypes were also produced in the Bauhaus workshops and mass produced for home and industrial use. Marianne Brandt's *Wandarm* of 1927, originally designed for hospital use, is a remarkable example, as is the more cumbersome extendable wall light by Karl Jucker.

Lighting was to be one of the major success stories of the Dessau Bauhaus, as regards both design and manufacture. Contracts were drawn up with major manufacturers, the most enduring of which was with Körting & Matthiesen (Kandem) in 1928. The Bauhaus acted as design consultants for Kandem, developing prototype designs, revising those already produced by the firm, and even (in 1932) setting up a Bauhaus competition to design a logo for the firm. By 1931 this collaboration of art and technology had resulted in sales of over 50,000 lights, a major source of income for the Bauhaus and a decisive factor in its growing economic independence. In the context of the burgeoning German lighting industry during the brief period of economic stability which ended in 1929, Bauhaus designs were to play a major part.

Other products of the metal workshop tended to suffer in comparison with this success and manufacturers for tableware were difficult to find. The ironic consequence of this was that the Bauhaus was still producing exclusive handcrafted designs well into the Dessau period.

Left Marianne Brandt, pendant ceiling light, c.1928. Bauhaus Archiv, Berlin. Brandt joined the Bauhaus in 1924 as a student. She is best known for her adjustable metal lamps, but also painted and made witty and imaginative photomontages.

The 1923 Exhibition

By 1923 the Thuringian government was beginning to exert pressure on Gropius to call the State Bauhaus to give an account of its activities. Gropius was at first unwilling to do this, as an earlier public display of Bauhaus work in 1919 had attracted adverse comment and further exacerbated an already uneasy situation between the School and certain factions in Weimar, who believed that state monies were being wasted on 'the Cathedral of Socialism' and that its lack of productivity was an affront. The annual Werkbund conference, however, which would naturally provide a sympathetic audience, was planned to take place in Weimar in this year and proved to be too good a chance to miss.

All the resources of the Bauhaus were directed toward the exhibition, which lasted from August 15 to September 30 1923, and the week of special events that went with it. The exhibition was a landmark in Bauhaus history, attracting some 15,000 visitors to Weimar from all over Europe. The publicity campaign to raise international awareness concerning the Bauhaus and its work was started a full six months before, and ranged in scope from articles in learned journals to advertising in cinemas. Gropius directed his considerable energies and extensive network of influential contacts to making the occasion a major arena in which to enhance the Bauhaus' standing.

The event was attended by such luminaries as the De Stijl architect J-J P Oud, whose presence marked a new unity between the Bauhaus and the Dutch movement. There was a lecture programme in which Gropius publicly declared his rejection of the romanticism of his original utopian manifesto by the very title of his keynote address, 'Art and Technology: a New Unity'.

Presentations of new works by Hindemith and Busoni, and Stravinsky's *The Soldier's Tale* performed in the composer's presence, added an international avant-garde musical dimension to 'Bauhaus Week'. Schlemmer's *Triadic Ballet* and *Mechanical Ballet* were both performed and there was also a ballet by Kandinsky. The rich diversity of experiences on offer during Bauhaus Week also included architectural displays, scientific films and performances by the Bauhaus Jazz Band.

In the main Bauhaus building the opportunity was taken to produce a major series of wall-paintings for public display. Oskar Schlemmer wrote:

That vestibule (of the van de Velde building) cries out for creative shaping. It could become the trademark of the Bauhaus . . . we shall combine wall painting with sculpture, displaying them in a context which normally seldom presents itself.

Schlemmer's own designs used semi-abstract human figures in the earth colors familiar from his easel paintings. His murals, along with others produced by the wall-painting workshop, were destroyed in 1930, on the orders of the School's then Nazi Director. A pro-

Below The sculpture workshop at Weimar in 1923. Bauhaus Archiv, Berlin. Work in hand by Oskar Schlemmer and others can be seen in the photograph.

gramme of restoration began in the late 1970s. The author of the influential *Mechanization Takes Command*, Siegfried Giedion, wrote of his reactions to the occasion of Bauhaus Week:

I gazed into a world newly forming . . . for the first time I got a universal insight into the cosmos of contemporary art. Those who took part in that event carry the impression of it all their lives.

In the view of the growing right-wing opposition toward the continuance of the Bauhaus at Weimar, however, there is no doubt that the exhibition helped hasten the school's departure. But even more significantly, the exhibition provided a focus and common purpose for all within the Bauhaus. What might have been a crisis for Gropius and the School proved a stimulus; hence the extraordinary fact that, when the Bauhaus left Weimar, its staff and student body survived virtually intact.

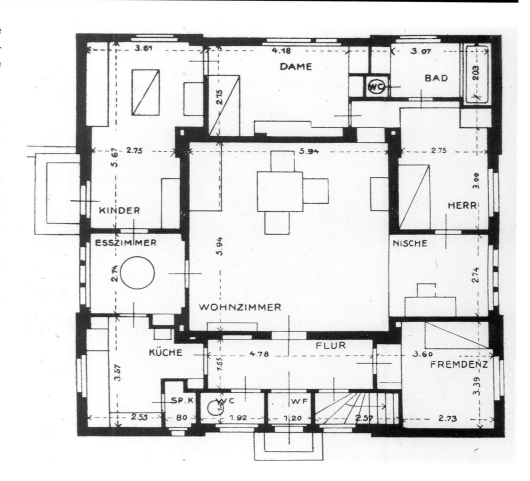

Below Walter Gropius (center) with Wassily Kandinsky (on the left in spectacles) and the Dutch architect J-J P Oud, photographed at the opening of the Bauhaus Exhibition in 1923. Bauhaus Archiv, Berlin.

Right Ground plan of the Haus am Horn, 1923. Bauhaus Archiv, Berlin. This experimental house, designed by Georg Muche for mass production using modern materials and construction methods, was a key feature of the 1923 Exhibition.

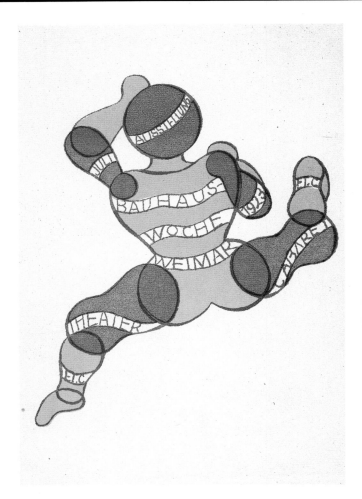

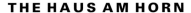

THE HAUS AM HORN

A key feature of the exhibition and one that created a great deal of comment was the collaborative venture, the experimental Haus am Horn, called after the street on which it was built (on the site of the Bauhaus vegetable patch). The one-family house, designed for mass-production using modern materials and construction methods, was a student initiative; there was no architecture department until four years later, after the move to Dessau. The chosen design was by the tutor Georg Muche, who considered himself primarily a painter. Although the design of the house was Muche's (he was about to marry and regarded the design as an opportunity to realize a 'dream house'), technical expertise was provided by Gropius' partner in his private architectural practice, Adolf Meyer. Gropius was to describe the aim of the house as attempting to achieve:

The greatest comfort with the greatest economy by the application of the best craftsmanship and the best distribution of space in form, size and articulation. In each room function is important, for example the kitchen is the most practical and simple of kitchens but it is not possible to use it as a dining room as well. Each room has its own definite character which suits its purpose.

The house, which has since been altered out of all recognition, was cuboid in shape, constructed of steel and concrete on one level apart from the central 20-foot high communal room, which was lit by clerestory windows, rising a story above the rest of the house. Each room was designed for a specific purpose. The children's playroom, for example, had a child-high wainscot of blue, yellow and red chalkboard to write on, and access to the room was through the mother's bedroom. The materials used throughout were practical, labor-saving and industrially produced, with rubber and linoleum flooring and Torfoleum (a patented form of compressed peat) panels providing insulation.

The furniture and fittings throughout the house were provided by the Bauhaus workshops. Furniture designs were by Marcel Breuer and others, lighting by the metal workshop, pottery was from Dornburg, and textiles by the weaving workshop. Muche and his design team insisted that each room-space be limited to its prescribed function. Thus the kitchen was intended only for the preparation of food; its design (by Benita Otte and Ernst Gebhard) is severely functional, intended (as was the rest of the house) to be managed by the woman of the house alone, without the help of domestic servants, at a time of stringent economic recession. The hygienic work surfaces, together with the logical ergonomic arrangement of the working space, made this a radical, even revolutionary, design. The pottery and glassware were Bauhaus designs and the

Opposite below Theodore Bogler, lidded flour container as used in the Haus am Horn kitchen. Kunstsammlungen zu Weimar.

ceramic storage jars were already in industrial production, as was some of the glass. Heinrich König, who wrote widely on modern industrial form, and was instrumental in fostering the move of the Bauhaus to Dessau, was to write of the kitchen:

But who remembers that it was the first kitchen in Germany with separated lower cupboards, suspended cupboards attached to the walls, a continuous work surface between them and the main work space in front of the window (there was no table in the middle of the kitchen)?

The Haus am Horn received a mixed critical reception. The Administrator of Federal Art Institutions, Dr Edwin Redslob, wrote that the house would, in his opinion, have:

Far-reaching cultural and economic consequences . . . the plight in which we find ourselves as a nation necessitates our being the first of all nations to solve the new problem of building. These plans go far toward blazing a new trail.

Gropius had hoped to persuade industrial manufacturers to donate materials for the Haus am Horn.

However the economic situation was such that Adolf Sommerfeld (for whom the Bauhaus had designed a radically different villa three years before) provided the money, and the house had to be sold privately the following year in the light of the Bauhaus' worsening financial situation. Indeed Gropius' efforts to provide international financial backing for the exhibition as a whole were not a success – even the day-to-day cleaning of the various exhibition sites had to be done by the wives of the tutorial staff.

1923 was a period of raging inflation. On July 1, the month before the exhibition's opening, the dollar was worth 160,000 marks, and by November 20 it was worth the extraordinary figure of 4,200,000,000,000 marks! Inevitably currency reform followed; the Dawes plan of early 1924 helped stabilize the German economy until the Wall Street crash of 1929. These few years of relative stability were to be the background to the Bauhaus' success at Dessau with design for mass production.

The exhibition marked a vital turning-point in the history of the Bauhaus. The artefacts on display and the revelation of Bauhaus methods established the School as a focal point for the avant-garde in Europe. However the converse of this was that increasingly violent attacks from the local Weimar press were now supported by the growing power of reactionary Nationalist critics throughout Germany.

Gropius, aware of the danger, suppressed an essay by Schlemmer on *Form and Function* which made use of the term 'Cathedral of Socialism' to describe the Bauhaus. Despite this there was an increase in attacks such as those of the right-wing critic K N Nonn, who mounted a sustained and virulent polemic against Gropius and the Bauhaus in a series of articles, the most notorious of which appeared in the Berlin newspaper *Deutsche Zeitung* in April 1924, entitled 'The State Garbage Supplies: The Staatliche Bauhaus in Weimar'. This evoked Weimar's most famous writer Goethe (whose work, which included *Faust*, had an almost mythic status in Germany), in its attack on the:

Mephistophelean spirit of negation, which has been its (the Bauhaus') distinguishing mark since 1919. What the Bauhaus offered in these first public displays stands so far beyond the pale of any kind of art that it can only be evaluated pathologically. A small band of interested persons, who for the most part are foreigners, should not be allowed to suffocate the healthy mass of youthful German art students like a layer of oil on clear water.

Whatever the problems of the exhibition's reception in Weimar, there is no question of its unifying impact on the entire Bauhaus and the boost it gave to staff and student morale. High morale was needed as never before, as political unrest worsened in the face of burgeoning inflation. In the last weeks of the Bauhaus Exhibition, in September 1923, the Thuringian government commissioned one and two million mark notes and a one billion mark note. The size of the denominations is indicative of the unprecedented financial situation, as is Bauhaus student Herbert Bayer's elegant design, a triumph of modernist minimalism in a field where normally complexity is essential to prevent forgery. Bayer's banknote designs are a potent signifier of the worthlessness of the currency.

On November 23 1923 Gropius' flat was subject to a military search; he was under suspicion of being a left-

wing sympathizer, although nothing incriminating could be found. In December Weimar was put under martial law, and troops were paraded in the streets to quell any civil disobedience. At the end of the year the government fell. The Bauhaus' days at Weimar were now numbered.

Above Wilhelm Wagenfeld, sauceboat, 1924, German silver with ebony handles. Bauhaus Archiv, Berlin.

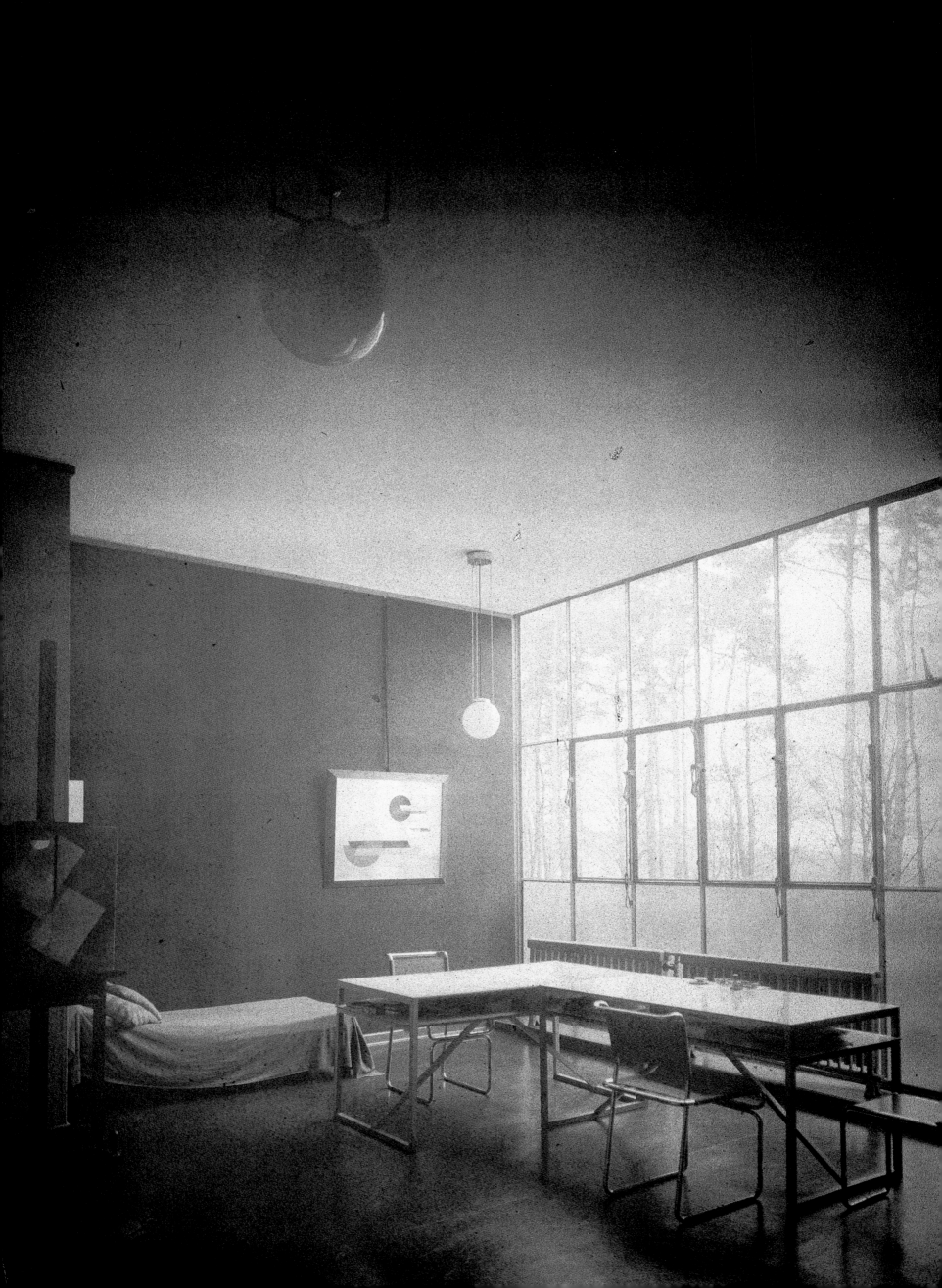

7

The Move to Dessau

The exhibition of 1923 focused European attention on the Bauhaus. The Circle of Friends of the Bauhaus, whose governing body included such celebrities as Albert Einstein, Arnold Schönberg, Peter Behrens and Marc Chagall, was formed in an effort to raise support and funds. However such moves, together with the international circulation of the Bauhaus Books, which made Bauhaus ideas available to a still wider public, served also to exacerbate Nationalist criticism within Germany of the Bauhaus' 'Internationalism'. Thus when a right-wing Nationalist government was returned early in 1924, it was inevitable that state funds should be withdrawn from the Bauhaus and staff given notice. By the end of 1924, a period of confusion for the Bauhaus, Gropius announced that the School would be dissolved when staff contracts expired in the following spring. Most of the teaching team agreed to stay together, although Christian Dell from the metal workshop and Adolf Meyer, Gropius' architectural partner, found other work. William Wagenfeld from the metal workshop also left to pursue his career elsewhere.

Dessau, the town which made the most positive proposal to house the Bauhaus, was radically different from Weimar in several important respects. A key industrial town in a mining area that also contained one quarter of Germany's chemical industry, Dessau's major manufacturing industry was the production of Junkers airplanes. The industrial character of Dessau, together with its comparative nearness to Berlin, made it a compelling site for the reformed Bauhaus. It was, however, the political character of the town above all that decided the matter. Dessau was a Social Democratic stronghold in a period of rampant Nationalism. The town's Mayor, Fritz Hesse, managed to persuade the City Council to vote considerable funds for the radical Bauhaus, which was viewed as a political refugee from right-wing Weimar. These grants were increased yearly and, together with the increasing income from workshop production (in the year 1926-27 the workshops made a net profit of 15,000 marks) ensured the security of the Bauhaus in a manner unthinkable in the Weimar years. Hesse also managed to ensure that the existing Dessau School of Arts and Crafts was to be maintained and Gropius was to become (at least in title) head of both this and the Bauhaus. The latter hope was not realized, however, and in 1926 the Bauhaus took an additional title 'Hochschule für Gestaltung' (Institute of Design) to distinguish its aims from those of the School of Arts and Crafts.

The first four years of the Bauhaus at Dessau until the Wall Street Crash of 1929 were, after the years of crippling inflation, a period of relative economic stability throughout Germany with the aid of American investment. Mayor Hesse's support was a vital factor in the Bauhaus' success, and in return the status of Dessau

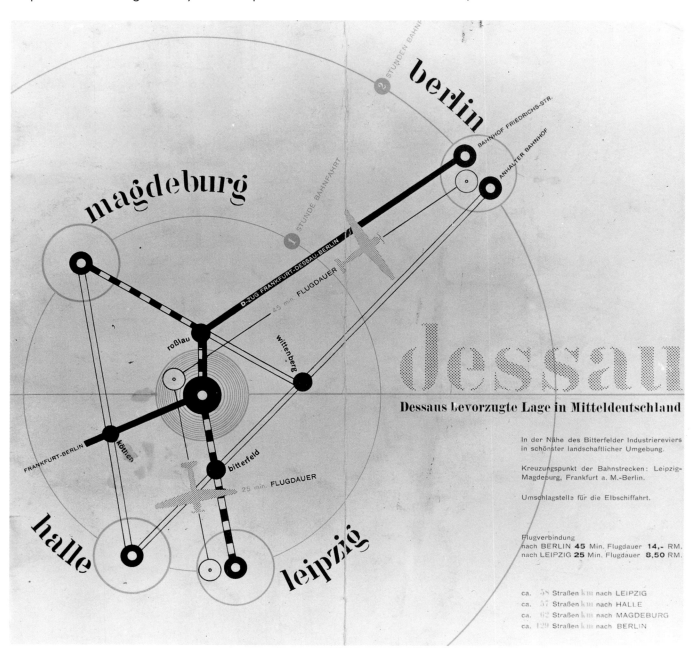

Right Joost Schmidt, prospectus for the Dessau tourist office 1930. Bauhaus Archiv, Berlin. Dessau was a key industrial town with a very different political character from that of Weimar.

Left Gerrit Rietveld, the Schröder House, Utrecht, plastered brick, concrete, iron and other materials. Centraal Museum, Utrecht, © DACS 1991. The Dessau Bauhaus was designed along similar lines and intended as a manifesto of architectural modernism.

Below Walter Gropius and Adolf Meyer, Fagus shoe-last factory Alfeld-an-der Leine, 1911. Bauhaus Archiv, Berlin. The influence of both this and Rietveld's De Stijl house can be seen in the design of the Bauhaus buildings at Dessau.

Above Joost Schmidt, prospectus design for the state tourist office, Dessau, 1931. Bauhaus Archiv, Berlin. The relationship between the municipal government and the Bauhaus was a close one.

Dessau, new buildings were clearly needed. Space was made available for both the School and Masters' dwellings on the edge of the town, and the building of the School began in summer 1925. It was in active use by October 1926, its speedy completion evidence of the efficacy of the building methods and materials employed in its making. Although it had been clear from the very inception of the Bauhaus that its ultimate aim was 'the building', it is an ironic fact that despite this, and the great interest at all times among both staff and students in matters architectural, there was no formal training in architecture until 1927. Projects such as the experimental Haus am Horn were realized with the professional advice of Adolf Meyer, Gropius' partner in his private architectural practice.

The complex of Bauhaus buildings, though fitted out in its entirety with designs from the Bauhaus workshops, was designed by Gropius and his architectural practice as a manifesto of architectural Modernism or, as it was termed in Germany and elsewhere at the time, the New Architecture. New Architects, who at this period included such pioneers as Frank Lloyd Wright, Le Corbusier and the De Stijl architect Gerrit Rietveld as well as Gropius himself, were engaged in debate concerning such concepts as architectural 'truth' and 'democracy'. The design of their buildings signified these qualities by various characteristics. For example, the structure of the building had to be expressed by its exterior appearance, as in Gropius' 1911 experimental Fagus factory. The democratic spirit of such buildings was signified by the lack of emphasis on one facade, which in older buildings had always been the entrance facade, at what was now regarded as the expense of others. The buildings could only be experienced in their entirety by walking around them, as Gropius said of the Bauhaus building, 'in order to understand its form and the function of its component parts'. The function of the component parts of the Bauhaus building can now best be appreciated by the aerial perspective offered by models, or from the contemporary air photographs commissioned by Gropius.

was enhanced by its association with Bauhaus products, which were to appear in ever-increasing numbers at trade fairs and exhibitions throughout Germany and the rest of the world. Visitors were soon to flock to Dessau to view the Bauhaus buildings and the Masters' Houses. Indeed Hesse's own fortunes became inextricably bound up with the Bauhaus, and his continued support for the School was a prime charge when the Nazis drove the Dessau Social Democrats from power in 1932.

Although staff and students had temporary working and living accommodation made available to them in

Right The Bauhaus, Dessau, dining room, 1925/26. Bauhaus Archiv, Berlin. The black and white folding doors at the rear lead to the stage area. Furniture is by Marcel Breuer, lighting by the metal workshop and color scheme by the mural painting workshop.

Left The Bauhaus, Dessau, staircase in the teaching block, 1925/26. Bauhaus Archiv, Berlin. The steps and upper surface of the parapet are of black and white terrazzo slabs.

New Architecture was also characterized by its use of modern materials, its emphasis on horizontal planes and the angular interlocking of part to part. The block-like appearance was further emphasized by the *sine qua non* of New Architecture, the flat roof. This, together with the white rendering of all or part of the exterior, was a major affront to conservative opinion. In Germany, as in other European countries, a pitched roof was held to represent tradition and nationality. In Weimar, criticism of the modest Haus am Horn concentrated on its perceived resemblance to an Arab hut or public convenience.

The complex of Bauhaus buildings was also radical in structure, with a reinforced concrete skeleton and the flat roofs of the buildings insulated with a layer of Torfoleum, a form of compressed peat used in the Haus am Horn. The insulation caused problems over such a large area and the roofs were prone to leakage. The new building served many purposes and was housed in a series of interlocking blocks, all of which could be reached under cover. The complex contained workshops, teaching and administration areas, the canteen, the theater, 28 units of student living accommodation, a gymnasium and Gropius' architectural practice, which was, after 1927, to become the Architecture Department.

For the students, the integration of living and working spaces fostered an extraordinary spirit of com-

Left The Bauhaus, Dessau, canteen, 1925/26. Bauhaus Archiv, Berlin. At both Weimar and Dessau the canteen served as a focus of social life, until the more rigorous regime initiated by Hannes Meyer on his appointment as Director in 1928.

munity. Xanti Schawinsky, who occupied one of the student rooms — which have served as a model for such accommodation ever since — commented 'all you had to do was to step out on to your balcony and whistle'. The cantilevered balconies (and indeed the roof garden at the top of the student block) were also prized amenities and form a striking feature of many of the photographs of the period.

The glass-walled workshop area, which revealed both the structure of the building and the activity within it, was the most striking feature of the exterior and the one significantly to have BAUHAUS emblazoned on its side. The structural principle of a glass curtain wall which hid nothing of the activity behind it was a development on a huge scale of Gropius' earlier experimental Fagus factory. The symbolic significance of the

wall (the building was known locally as 'the Aquarium'), was not lost on the Nazis and the wall was bricked in when the Bauhaus was dissolved.

Gropius' design for the Bauhaus has become his best-known work, and its influence on public buildings since has been incalculable. In *The New Architecture and the Bauhaus* (published in 1935), Gropius wrote:

A modern building . . . must be true to itself, logically transparent and virginal of lies or trivialities, as befits a direct affirmation of our contemporary world of mechanization and rapid transit.

When the building was formally declared open on December 6 1926, in the presence of some thousand people, Gropius concluded his address with these words:

The more we succeed in working together in ever closer co-operation, the more we shall succeed, starting from this spiritual center, in establishing links between industry, the crafts, the sciences, and the creative forces of our time . . . First and foremost, this building has been created for our young people, for the creatively talented young people who some day will mold the face of our new world.

With the benefit of hindsight, Gropius' idealism, encapsulated in the term 'spiritual center' to describe the Bauhaus, seems almost unbearably poignant.

Dessau City Council, in addition to funding the Bauhaus buildings (which soon ran over budget), had also agreed to raise monies for a scheme for four housing units for Bauhaus Masters, some ten minutes' walk away. Each of the three pairs of semi-detached houses, occupied by Klee and Kandinsky, Muche and Schlemmer, Moholy-Nagy and Feininger and their families, together with the Director's detached house, shared certain characteristics with the public building, even to the glass wall in the entrance area – which Kandinsky had painted white to render it opaque.

As with the Haus am Horn, the Masters' Houses were designed on strictly functional lines to be run without the help of servants. As Gropius wrote, 'to build means to shape the activities of life. The organism of a house derives from the course of the activities which take place within it . . . '. He added, severely, 'the shape of the building is not there for its own sake'.

The houses were all designed for maximum efficiency; their functionality was built on the understanding that, as in the Haus am Horn, the families would service their own needs rather than make use of servants. Thus maximum use was made of fitted furniture, the windows were large to allow optimum light and fitted with blinds rather than curtains (thought to be fussy, and even unhygienic), and the houses were equipped throughout with labor-saving devices. The critic Max Osborn, writing in the liberal Berlin paper *Vossische Zeitung*, commented in December 1926:

With careful consideration every detail has been designed for practical use. The individual inhabitant is not forced into anything. Even though the halves of each of the twin houses are almost identical, they all look different. Everyone puts their own personality into them.

Osborn makes special mention of the use of color in the houses:

Walls painted gold and silver are not lacking in these homes, producing a most intriguing effect. [Black . . .] having been tested in paintings by Kandinsky and Moholy . . . has been discovered by the Bauhaus as a color for the home . . . all this integrates into a light-colored, unsentimental, clear and exceedingly wholesome setting for human existence and creative activity.

Gropius' own house became a showplace for Bauhaus ideas on building and interior design and was much visited by the curious from all over the world. The rooms show designs from all the Bauhaus workshops: furniture by Marcel Breuer, wall-hangings from the weaving workshop, even a set of tea-infusing spoons from the metal workshop. As the Haus am Horn had been, to a certain degree, the realization of Muche's dream of a family home so, to an even greater degree, was this Gropius' ideal home, demonstrating his dictum given in Volume 12 of the Bauhaus Books, *Bauhausbauten Dessau*:

Smooth and sensible functioning of daily life is not an end in itself, it merely constitutes the condition for achieving a maximum of personal freedom and independence. Hence the standardization of the practical processes of life does not mean new enslavement and mechanization of the individual, but rather frees life from unnecessary ballast in order to let it develop all the more richly and unencumbered.

The Institute of Design

In 1926 the original plan for the Bauhaus to amalgamate with the Dessau School of Arts and Crafts was abandoned and the Bauhaus took the title 'Hochschule für Gestaltung' (Institute of Design) to make the difference of function between it and the earlier Dessau institution perfectly plain. Institute of Design was no empty title and it signaled major institutional changes, not the least of which was the setting up of a system to deal with the marketing of Bauhaus products. This enterprise was known as the Bauhaus Corporation and the importance given to the venture can be gauged by the fact that its Business Manager's salary in the first year of its operation was second only to that of Gropius.

The original system of Masters of Form and Masters of Craft working together, which had been such a keystone of the Weimar years, was now abandoned. Craftsmen were employed to train students in technical matters but they no longer had the same status as the Form Masters, who were now known by the academic title of Professor. The system of apprentices and journeymen continued for a time, however, as did the system of external validation of students' work. Later in the Dessau period students worked toward an internally validated Bauhaus diploma and were no longer termed apprentices and journeymen in the medieval manner that had seemed appropriate at Weimar.

The abandoning of the team-teaching system had always seemed inevitable. It was rare if not unique for the system of Form Master and Craft Master to work as well as it had done at Dornburg with Gerhard Marcks and Max Krehan. Even this did not last; when the Bauhaus moved to Dessau it was decided, for reasons that are not clear, that the pottery should not continue in its Bauhaus form, and Krehan remained behind at Dornburg while Marcks moved to Dessau.

Gropius had always envisaged a time when Bauhaus-trained graduates could become tutors themselves. He intended that such graduates (who were self-evidently versatile and capable by the very nature of the rigorous Weimar system) should become Masters of Form and Workshop Masters in one: the so-called 'Young Masters'. These Young Masters, who were to include Herbert Bayer, Gunta Stölzl and Marcel Breuer, had a status quite distinct from that of Professors like Kandinsky and Klee and were to be paid two-thirds of the professorial salaries. The Young Masters were to pass on their skills to a new Bauhaus breed who could not be described as students, still less apprentices. These phenomena were described by Gropius as 'a new previously unavailable type of *collaborator for industry, craft and building* who is the master equally of technique *and* form'.

The workshops themselves were redefined at Dessau. Some, like the Dornburg pottery (which had always been geographically separate from the Bauhaus) continued as an independent enterprise. The stained glass workshop, which was prevented by its very nature from being anything but craft-based and had no possibility of collaborating with industry, did not continue at Dessau, although Josef Albers, who had directed it, was to play a vital part in shaping the new Bauhaus.

The metal and cabinet-making workshops were combined under the Young Master Marcel Breuer, whose own designs for furniture using metal tubing had first been made in the cabinet-making workshop; it was a logical step no longer to define the activity of the workshop by the materials it used. The function of each workshop had now become paramount and thus Breuer was in charge of a workshop with the re-established title of 'Interior Design' and the function of producing both fitted and free-standing furniture as well as a large range of household equipment.

The function of those other workshops moved to Dessau was also differentiated in their new and splendidly equipped premises. The printing workshop at Weimar had concentrated on the production of graphic art produced by traditional methods and

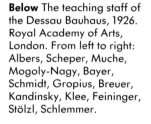

Below The teaching staff of the Dessau Bauhaus, 1926. Royal Academy of Arts, London. From left to right: Albers, Scheper, Muche, Mogoly-Nagy, Bayer, Schmidt, Gropius, Breuer, Kandinsky, Klee, Feininger, Stölzl, Schlemmer.

limited editions of books and journals. At Dessau, under the direction of another Young Master, Herbert Bayer, it became famous in its re-established form for its radical approach to typography in the widest sense and all manner of advertising products. As at Weimar, Schlemmer had charge of the theater workshop, while Muche continued the weaving workshop. Muche was assisted until his resignation in 1927 by Gunta Stölzl, herself a student at Weimar, who then took overall charge until 1931. The bookbinding workshop and the wood workshop were both discontinued and what had been the sculpture workshop under first Itten and then Schlemmer's direction was now termed the plastic workshop. From 1925-28 this was under the direction of another remarkable Young Master, famous today for his graphic and typographical work, Joost Schmidt.

Kandinsky and Klee continued their teaching as at Weimar, and their respective seminars on form and other special classes were a compulsory element of the course for all students. The *Vorkurs* was directed from 1923 to 1928 at Weimar and at Dessau by Moholy-Nagy and Josef Albers, and by Albers alone after Moholy's resignation in 1928. Albers (1888-1976) had come to the Weimar Bauhaus in 1920 as a mature student after qualifying elsewhere and working for some time as an art teacher in primary school education. One of the many facts that links Albers' and Itten's teaching is that they both applied methods of 'learning by doing', hitherto used with young children, to the teaching of adult students.

When Albers began his studies with Itten's basic course he was 31, the same age as his tutor. So evident was his skill, especially in the use of materials, that Gropius created a special post for him as a junior member of staff on the *Vorkurs*. He was even given his own independent teaching space in converted stables some distance from the main school. Here Albers taught the students the use of materials, a subject he continued teaching at Dessau, where he was formally appointed the first Young Master and taught the *Vorkurs* in conjunction with Moholy until 1928, then taking overall charge until 1931. From 1928-29 Albers was also in charge of what was now known as the department of interior design. At Weimar, and especially at Dessau, Albers and Moholy made a strong team, just what was required to bridge the gap between the subjectivity of Itten's approach and the demands of the new collaboration between art and industry.

Albers' preliminary course was imaginative and innovative. The *Bauhaüsler* Hannes Beckmann remembered that on the first day of the *Vorkurs* Albers arrived carrying a pile of newspapers, which he distributed among the students, instructing them:

We are poor, not rich. We can't afford to waste materials or time. We have to make the most out of the least. All art starts with a material and therefore we have to investigate what our material can do. Our studies should lead to constructive thinking.

The students were each to take a newspaper and 'try to make something out of them that is more than you have now'. Albers stressed the importance of respect for the material and of using it in a way that 'makes sense — preserve its inherent characteristics'. Having said this Albers then left the room. The students were, as Beckmann remembered, 'quite flabbergasted', but set to work. Some made 'boats, castles, airplanes, animals and all kinds of cute little figurines'. Albers dismissed all these as 'kindergarten products', which might as well have been made (and better made perhaps) in other materials. Much to the students' surprise, Albers seized on 'a study of extreme simplicity' by a Hungarian student of architecture, who had taken his newspaper and folded it lengthwise so that it stood up 'like a folding screen'. Albers explained how well the qual-

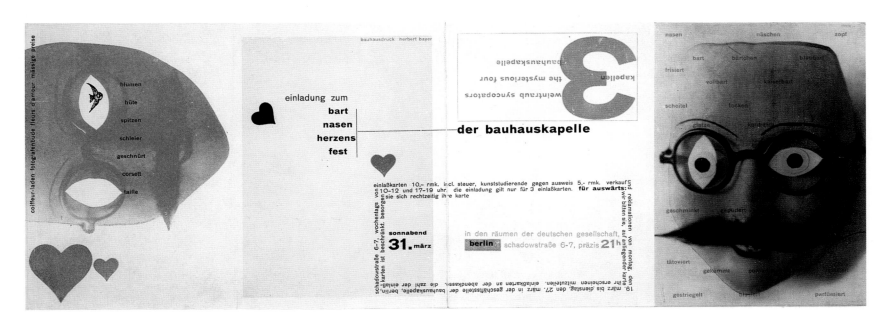

worked continuously at the Bauhaus for 13 years, a longer period of service than that of any other *Bauhaüsler*. He then went to teach at Black Mountain College, North Carolina, for the next 16 years and at other education establishments in the United States, until he was appointed Professor and Chairman of the Department of Design at Yale University in 1950. The direct dissemination of Bauhaus ideas from such a key figure as Albers has had a decisive effect on the history of American painting. Through Albers' paintings, his teaching, and his treatise on color theory published in 1963, *Interaction of Color*, he can be seen to have influenced a wide range of artists working in America in the 1950s and 1960s. His interest in optical illusion links him to Op Art, while his precise interest in form links him to such artists as Kenneth Noland, who studied at Black Mountain College.

Albers' *Homage to the Square* painting series was begun in 1949 and developed at Yale. As a painter Albers' lifetime study was the psychological impact of color; his interest in Gestalt psychology led him toward an exploration of the effects of optical illusion, as he phrased it:

The origin of art was the discrepancy between physical fact and psychic effect . . . choice of colors used, as well as their order, is aimed at an interaction — influencing and changing each other forth and back.

He evolved a series of color combinations to explore a consistent format of squares, applying the pigment directly from the tube.

The *Vorkurs* remained the indispensable prerequisite for further work at the Bauhaus. In the period from 1925 to 1929 at Weimar and Dessau, Albers taught the *Vorkurs* for the first semester and Moholy-Nagy for the second. Albers' course, as has already been indicated, concentrated on the examination of the nature of materials and the students worked with the simplest of materials, mostly paper and scissors, achieving extraordinarily varied results with minimal means in their experimental projects. A standard problem set for every student on Albers' course was that of construct-

Above Georg Muche, photograph of the Dessau furniture workshop reflected in a sphere, 1929. Bauhaus Archiv, Berlin. Muche and Moholy-Nagy were both much interested in photographic experimentation.

ities of the paper had been understood and used, and how the folding process was 'natural to paper'. Hannes Beckmann described how, through the introductory course:

A whole new world of seeing and thinking opened up to us . . . the *Vorkurs* was a kind of group therapy . . . seeing the solutions made by other students we learned quickly to recognize the most elegant solution to a given problem.

Albers encouraged his students to experiment with all manner of materials and emphasized the importance of economy in the use of materials. In this connection another student, T Lux Feininger, the son of the artist, remembered another exercise in three dimensions on Albers' Use of Materials course in which a student made 'a most impressive structure' composed entirely of spent razor blades 'which are slotted and punched by the manufacturer' and burnt wooden matchsticks.

Albers was to remain with the Bauhaus until its final closure in Berlin in 1933. As student and teacher he had

Right Eugen Batz, study of colors and forms from the course on form that Kandinsky taught at Dessau. Bauhaus Archiv, Berlin.

ing a working camera bellows out of paper by folding and cutting. No technical instruction was given and each student had to solve the problem independently. Such complex exercises with paper made students skilled in the solving of problems of surface and plane, essential preparation for future designers for industry as well as the builders of the New Architecture.

Moholy's second semester course was essentially concerned with training students to perceive three-dimensional relationships. To this end they were encouraged to experiment in developing constructions of metal, wood, string and other simple materials, in order to demonstrate the solution of such problems and, in Moholy's own words in *Material to Architecture*, Volume 14 of the Bauhaus Books:

Spatial design . . . and interweaving of spatial shapes, shapes that are ordered into certain well-defined, although invisible space relationships and which represent the fluctuating play of tension and forces.

The emphasis on spatial imagination, stressed by both Albers and Moholy, can be seen in its most dramatic form in Moholy's *Light/Space Modulator*. This extraordinary structure, a form of dynamic light sculpture, bears an obvious relationship both to the work Moholy was engaged in at this period with the students in the metal workshop, who were working on the range of lighting, and to his own paintings of this period. Moholy had long been fascinated by the properties of light, and sought to overcome the traditional limitations of painting in order to create a universal vocabulary which would elevate the perceptions. 'Constructive art is processual', he wrote, 'forever open in all directions. It is a builder of man's ability to perceive, to react emotionally and to reason logically.' Construction of the *Light/Space Modulator* occupied Moholy from 1922-30. Some 60 inches high, it is made of perforated metal discs, glass, plastic and wire mesh. All the materials are chosen for their qualities of transparency or translucency. In its stationary form it bears an obvious relationship to Moholy's paintings and graphic work. However, once the motor is switched on the object becomes transformed, as its component parts whirr into action to produce the most extraordinary light and shadow effects. Its impact must have been intensified when demonstrated to Moholy's students in its original setting of a small darkened room.

The moving abstract images produced by the *Light/Space Modulator* in motion were captured in a series of films made by Moholy in 1930-32. Moholy's pioneering activity with both photography and moving pictures was maintained and enriched throughout his period at the Bauhaus, and the *Light/Space Modulator* is but one facet of his extraordinarily varied yet consistent career as artist and educator.

At Dessau, as at Weimar, the *Vorkurs* was an essential prerequisite for further work for the student. Equally, a knowledge of the *Vorkurs* is essential for those who wish today to understand the many forms of Bauhaus activity and the concepts that governed them. The courses at Weimar and Dessau were as different as their respective course leaders, but certain key constants remained. The students continued to be encouraged to learn by doing, and spontaneity was encouraged. Exploration of the use of materials was still essential to the course at Dessau but the workshop became more like a research laboratory, exploring links

Left László Moholy-Nagy *The Light of the City*, 1926, photomontage. Bauhaus Archiv, Berlin.

Below Marianne Brandt *A Matter of Taste*, 1926, photomontage. Courtesy of Barry Friedmann Ltd. Under the influence of Moholy-Nagy and Muche, Brandt made lively and imaginative photomontages as well as her more familiar work in the metal workshop.

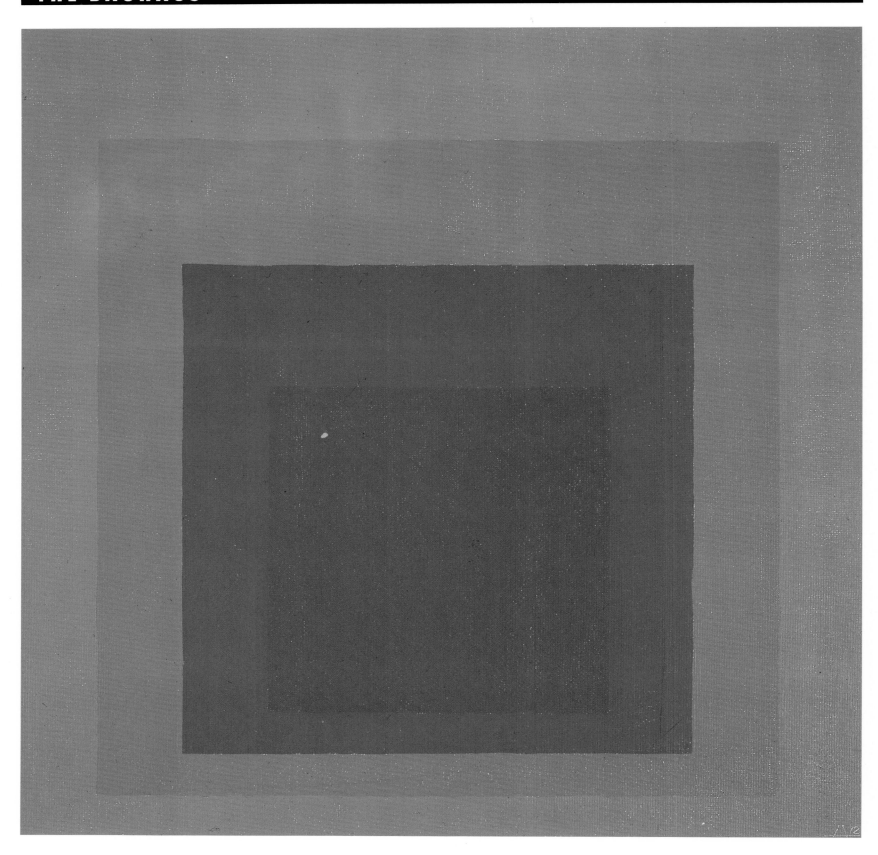

Above Josef Albers *Study for Homage to the Square* 1972, oil on masonite, 23⅞ × 23⅞ inches (60.6 × 60.6 cm). San Francisco Museum of Modern Art, gift of Anni Albers and the Josef Albers Foundation, © COSMOPRESS Geneva and DACS London 1991. Albers was the first Bauhaus student to be promoted to the rank of Young Master, and worked on the *Vorkurs* with Moholy-Nagy.

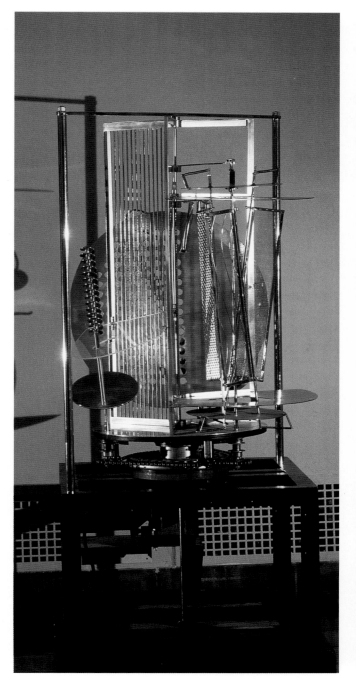

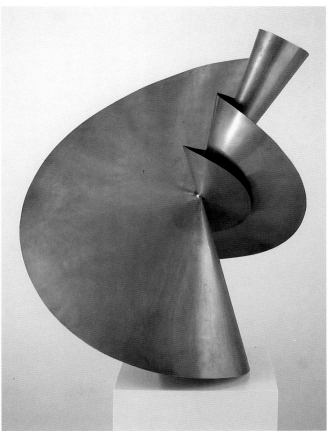

Above left László Moholy-Nagy *Light-Space Modulator* 1929/30, kinetic sculpture of steel, plastic, wood and other materials with electric motor, 59 × 27⅜ × 27⅜ inches (151.1 × 69.9 × 69.9cm). Courtesy of the Busch-Reisinger Museum, Harvard University, gift of Sybil Moholy-Nagy.

Above right László Moholy-Nagy *Construction* 1923. Courtesy of the Trustees of the British Museum, London.

between art and technology, than a crafts atelier in the medieval mode.

The training given on the *Vorkurs* and the general atmosphere at Dessau encouraged the students to develop a certain frame of mind, at the same time systematic and orderly and also experimental and intuitive: these characteristics are a linking feature which does much to explain the versatile work of an otherwise disparate range of Bauhaus alumni.

From 1928 there were pioneering courses, in the face of considerable opposition, in such studies as psychology and industrial management in order to further acquaint the students with the realities of life outside the Bauhaus. Despite the more obvious changes, however, and the general thrust toward the collaboration of art and technology on Moholy's taking over the course, *Vorkurs* teaching demonstrates a remarkable continuity of approach under Itten, Moholy and Albers, not least in the value placed on creative intuition within a framework of rigorous training.

Left Takehito Mizutani *Three-part Figure* 1928. Bauhaus Archiv, Berlin. An example of the experimental constructions to which the *Vorkurs* gave rise.

MEISTER DOPPELHÄUSER von unten gesehen . 1926. ARNDT

26 A

Public Architecture at Dessau

Left Alfred Arndt, color plans
for the Bauhaus Masters'
houses, Dessau 1926.
Bauhaus Archiv, Berlin.

One of the many ironies of the Bauhaus concerns the status of architecture. When it was established in 1919, the Bauhaus *Manifesto* stated that the *bau-haus* was the house where 'the final goal is the building'. Feininger's accompanying woodcut showed the *Cathedral of the Future*, and the Bauhaus *Programme* itself, inspired by the utopian idealism of Ruskin and Morris, declared that 'architects, painters and sculptors must once again learn to know and understand the multiform shape of buildings in their totality and their parts'. The Bauhaus was to train a 'new guild of craftsmen', to include architects as well as painters and sculptors, who were to discover the way 'back to the crafts'.

The *Programme* went on to include the 'common planning of large utopian architectural designs' in its hopes for the immediate future. Nearly two years later, the Bauhaus Statutes contain mention of architectural matters in only two of fifteen paragraphs, and even there the references are to architecture as one of a number of studies, as in 'the teaching of shapes (drawing, painting, modelling, building)' and 'accurate draftsmanship and the making of models' for all three-dimensional shapes (objects for use, furniture, rooms, buildings).

While Gropius himself remained in architectural practice, the only major building of the early Weimar years built with the collaboration of the Bauhaus workshops was the Sommerfeld House, of 1921, generally thought at the time to have been an Expressionist aberration from the architect of the pioneering Fagus factory, with its rational, severely cubic form and radical use of glass. By 1922, however, Gropius was warning his staff (in a Memorandum in February) against the 'danger of excessive Romanticism', 'a misunderstood Rousseauvian return to Nature', and was beginning to urge a new direction to become encapsulated in the title of his keynote address at the Bauhaus Exhibition in Weimar the following year 'Art and Technology: A New Unity'.

Building appeared in the Bauhaus programme but not on the teaching curriculum. When the Bauhaus Exhibition of 1923 was being planned, the experimental Haus am Horn was a student-led initiative, designed by the painter and master of the weaving workshop, Georg Muche, and built with the aid of Gropius' partner of the Fagus factory, Adolf Meyer. The collaborative venture of the Haus am Horn, and the international interest the house aroused, intensified the desire among students and staff to have architectural

Right Johannes Itten *The House of the White Man* 1920, lithograph. Courtesy of the Trustees of the British Museum, London. This print illustrates the Cubist-inspired style of modernist architecture that Gropius developed on a far grander scale at Dessau.

Left The Bauhaus, Dessau. Bauhaus Archiv, Berlin. This photograph of the 1977 restoration of the Bauhaus buildings was taken in 1988.

Below Alfred Arndt, plans for the upper story of the Auerbach house in Jena, designed by Gropius and Meyer in 1924. Bauhaus Archiv, Berlin.

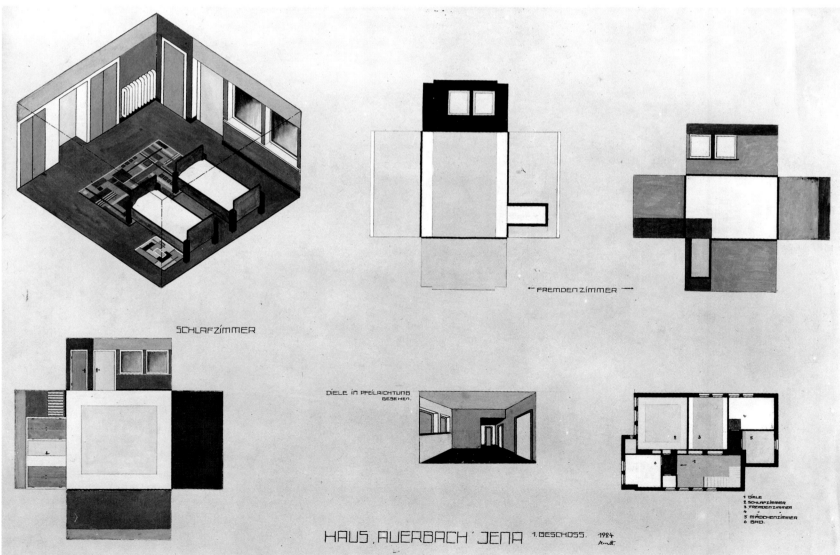

SCHLAFZIMMER

FREMDEN ZIMMER

DIELE IN PFEILRICHTUNG GESEHEN.

HAUS , AUERBACH , JENA   1. GESCHOSS.   1924

Above Hajo Rose *Highjumping* 1930, photograph. Bauhaus Archiv, Berlin. The Dessau student block with its cantilevered balconies can be seen in the background.

1924 with Muche and Marcel Breuer as its leading participants. Muche designed a 15-story concrete-built block of apartments and Breuer designed a much lower block. Gropius himself with Meyer's collaboration projected a set of models for industrially made housing. These took the form of industrially constructed box units which could be put together in various ways. Gropius and Meyer termed the housing units 'largescale building bricks'.

The move to Dessau in 1925 necessitated the building of new premises and staff houses, work undertaken by Gropius' private practice with the collaboration of the School. The Bauhaus buildings were regarded as classics of international Modernism, but there was still as yet no department of architecture at what had now become the Bauhaus Institute of Design. Gropius was convinced that students could only deal with problems relating to architecture by being thoroughly prepared with a grounding in craft and design skills before proceeding to a specialized architectural course. A change of heart came soon after the arrival in Dessau, however, and when the students proceeded to the Department of Architecture which was eventually set up in 1927 (with equal status to that of the workshops, taking over the space originally allocated to Gropius' private practice), it was direct from the preliminary course without training in craft skills.

Some important housing projects were, however, realized to Gropius' design with the participation of the School in the years before the eventual setting up of the Department of Architecture in 1927 and Gropius' resignation a year later to concentrate on his private practice. The Törten estate, Dessau, built in three stages of construction during the years 1926, 1927 and 1928, represented an important stage in the Bauhaus' development. Whereas the Bauhaus buildings and the Masters' Houses had been financed by the Dessau City

matters given greater importance at the Bauhaus. Nothing was built while the school was at Weimar, although an architectural working group was set up in

Right The Gropius House, Lincoln, Mass, designed by Walter Gropius in 1938. This was the first modern house in the area; Gropius' appointment as chairman of the Architecture Department at Harvard ensured the success of the International style he championed at the Bauhaus.

Council, the Törten estate was built with money from the state, a public commission of considerable importance in response to the pressing need for rationalized low-cost housing for working families.

Though small, the apartments (which were arranged in various forms, the great majority in two-story terraces) were planned to high standards, with central heating, fitted cupboards and double glazing. The plots on which the officially termed 'homesteads' stood were of generous size, as they were intended to be used as allotments on which tenants could grow their own food, and each had outbuildings in which small farm animals could be kept. The project as a whole was conceived in semi-rural terms; the tenants could be offered the means of attaining a measure of self-sufficiency and also possibly supplement their incomes by the sale of their own produce. The estate contained a co-operative store, with flats above it, built as an integral part of the development.

As an evolved form of Gropius' early projects for largescale building bricks, Törten was constructed from components made largely on site in several rigorously timetabled phases, with resulting savings on labor and transport costs. Three hundred units were constructed between 1926 and 1928 and a further five blocks, consisting of 28 flats, were completed in 1930. The 'National Homesteads Housing Development', as it was officially known, was strictly rationalized in its planning and production, the very timetable of building used was, according to Gropius, 'similar to the ones used by railroads'. The site was chosen because its sand and gravel could be used to make a concrete mix to construct the units. As Gropius himself explained in *Bauhausbauten Dessau*, he decided to use:

A method of concrete construction according to my own system, keeping the amount of material to be moved to the

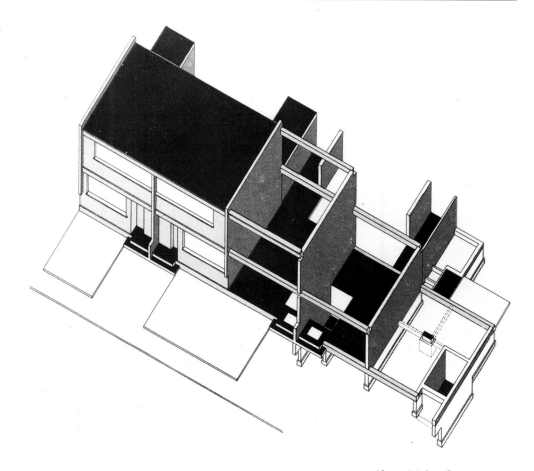

construction site low, for the presence of sand and gravel requires no more than the transport of cement and cinder to the site for the manufacture of the cinder concrete wall units . . . the principle of work at the site was to re-use the same man for the same phase of the construction in each block of houses and thereby increase output.

The venture was a collaborative one in Bauhaus terms, although the commission was given to Gropius, and represented an important summary of Bauhaus

Above Walter Gropius, construction plan for the state homesteads on the Törten Estate, 1926. Bauhaus Archiv, Berlin. Although commissioned from Gropius, the venture was a collaborative one and represented an important summary of Bauhaus ideas at the time.

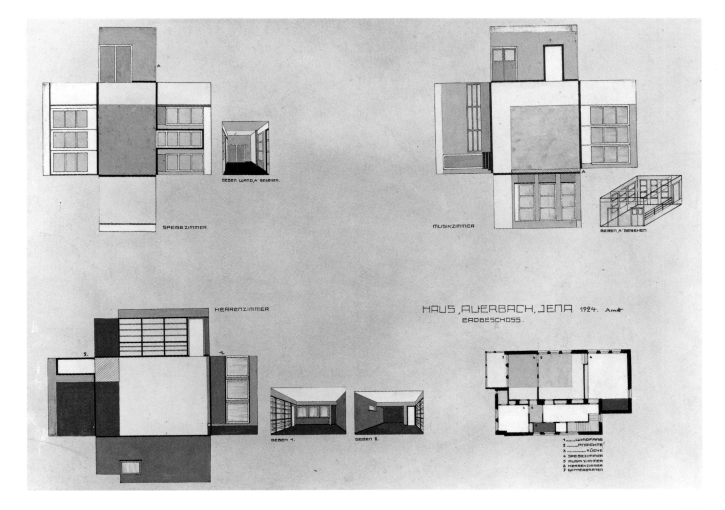

Left Alfred Arndt, color plans for Gropius and Meyer's Auerbach House, Jena, 1924. Bauhaus Archiv, Berlin.

ideas at the time on the subject of public housing; a
process that had begun with the Haus am Horn, which
was conceived as a single-family home for a middle-
class family and was originally planned for replication
as a mass housing project. The Törten homesteads may
also be seen as a strictly rationalized low-cost mass-
produced complement to the individual Masters'
Houses in Dessau.

Unfortunately the scheme was dogged with difficulties almost from the beginning, in some measure due to
the scale of the operation (which was larger than anything tackled by the Bauhaus before), and faults began
to show up on the buildings relatively quickly. Many
have been adapted and some restored so that some
idea may still be obtained of the original state of the
buildings.

The homesteads attracted a great deal of adverse
criticism, of a kind only too familiar from the Weimar
days. As with the Haus am Horn, the flat roofs were
decried by Nationalist critics as 'non-German', and the
houses were compared to 'concrete stables' and 'dog
kennels' in the Dessau papers. The radical rationalization of the building process itself was seen as a
threat to traditional methods of craftsmanship.

In Dessau itself Gropius designed a labor office as an entry for a competition in 1927. It was built between 1928 and 1929 of brown-toned brick on a semicircular steel skeleton and is the only building designed by Gropius in Dessau to have survived virtually intact. It was designed to be strictly functional, aiming to facilitate the servicing of a constant flow of many people seeking work. The inner section of the semicircle was toplit from skylights and to this one-story structure Gropius added a two-story administration building. Gropius explained his aims in devising:

... the semicircular form of the floor plan enabling the deployment of the large waiting rooms – divided into segments according to vocational groups – at the periphery, and the individual counselling offices on the other hand behind them in the interior.

The other building which survives from this period, although not in nearly as good a state, is an experimental steel house designed by Georg Muche as his final venture into matters architectural. This was constructed on the edge of the Törten estate, which served for some years as an arena for Bauhaus architectural experiments. Muche explained his thinking thus:

The customary house is built on a floor plan, fixed in the organization of its rooms ... but the family is a flexible organism ... hence the floor plan must be worked out in such a way that enlargement or diminution is possible as a natural arrangement without having to demolish building units.

The house was built in 1927 to a design by Muche and Richard Paulick, from prefabricated steel sheets on a steel frame with a concrete foundation. The manufacturers projected it as a model for such purposes as holiday homes; its major advantage was that such houses could be constructed far quicker even than normal prefabricated units. Muche himself was to leave

Left Walter Gropius photographed in the USA in 1935, shortly before his appointment to Harvard.

his work at the Bauhaus in the year of the house's construction to join the teaching staff of the school Itten had founded in Berlin, still convinced that 'the residence which can be added on to and which has a flexible floor plan is a requisite of our era'.

Left Walter Gropius, Emery Roth & Sons and Pietro Belluschi, Pan Am Building, New York City, 1958-63. This was the last building on which Gropius collaborated.

The Weaving Workshop

Left The weaving workshop
at Dessau in 1927, with one
of the 'weaving women'.
Bauhaus Archiv, Berlin. The
adjustable lighting was
designed by Marianne
Brandt and Hans Przyrembel.

Right A woven striped cover by Suze Ackerman of 1923/24. Kunstsammlungen zu Weimar.

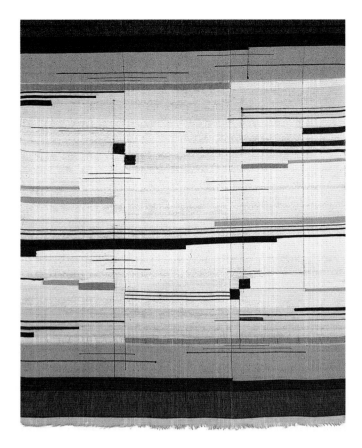

Georg Muche was Master of Form in the weaving workshop from 1921-27 at both Weimar and Dessau, combining his duties at Weimar with teaching on the *Vorkurs*. He was by far the youngest teacher at the Weimar Bauhaus and he made it clear from the beginning that he was not interested in the techniques of weaving but only in painting. Muche's independence and his *laissez-faire* attitude toward the technical activity of the weaving workshop had its advantages. The students evolved a distinctive style at Weimar which made the products of the textiles workshop second only to those of the ceramics workshop in terms of commissions and sales.

For the first year of the Bauhaus' existence at Weimar, raw materials were in very short supply. This scarcity forced the students working with textiles into ingenious solutions, utilizing even small scraps of material collected from the people of Weimar. The workshop's first major commission, the decorative hangings for the Sommerfeld House, were made from appliqué scraps, in geometric designs echoing the carved wall treatments and the overall design of the internal fittings of the house.

The designs of Bauhaus textiles at Weimar were particularly linked with the work being done on the *Vorkurs*; indeed Muche was Itten's assistant for part of the course, and on leaving the Bauhaus in 1927 joined the staff of Itten's own school of art in Berlin. For a period, until 1921, the *Vorkurs* was taught separately to male and female students. There was much discussion at Weimar among staff and students alike as to whether certain 'heavy' crafts such as metalwork and furniture-making were suitable for women, whereas weaving and work with textiles generally was felt to be historically validated as a traditionally female domain. The first adverse reactions to Marianne Brandt in the metal workshop by her male fellow students will be remembered in this connection, and such gender distinctions in craft production can still be found today.

During the period in which the Basic Course students were divided by gender, the teaching in the so-called Women's Department *(Frauenabteilung)* of the *Vorkurs* stressed sensitivity in the use of materials, 'observation' and contrasting textures and forms, qualities which can be perceived in student studies by Gunta Stölzl, including a drawing of a thistle. Another more complex landscape study of 1920 has angular forms of fir trees and telegraph poles contrasted with undulating hills and rivers. Similarly contrasting values can be seen in the tapestry made in the same year by one of the male apprentices, Max Peiffer-Watenphul, which was woven as a leaving present for Itten and uses strong

Below Max Peiffer-Watenphul's split-gobelin of 1921 shows the influence of the *Vorkurs* in its use of geometric forms. Bauhaus Archiv, Berlin. It was woven as a tribute to Itten and given him as a farewell present by the students when he left the Bauhaus in October 1922.

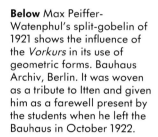

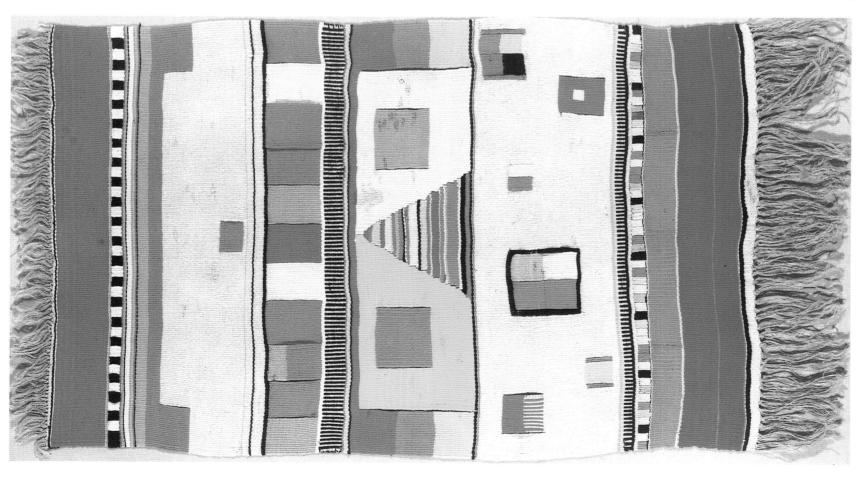

Above A wallhanging by Ida Kerkovius made from felt appliqué, 1921. Bauhaus Archiv, Berlin. The appliqué forms are similar to those used in the textiles for the Sommerfeld House.

primary colors and basic geometric forms. Helen Nonné-Schmidt, wife of Bauhaus Master Joost Schmidt, who worked in the weaving workshop at this period, described the particular qualities of women as weavers:

The artistically active woman applies herself most often and most successfully to work in a two-dimensional plane . . . weaving represents the fusion of an infinite multiplicity to unity, the interlocking of many threads to make up a fabric.

As with other workshops in the Weimar Bauhaus, shortages of material and vital equipment began to ease in 1921. The early years under Itten's tuition were, like the *Vorkurs* itself, a triumph of invention in response to necessity. Although the lack of looms made the teaching of orthodox textile techniques impossible, much work was done with textile appliqué, a technique used not only for such commissions as the Sommerfeld House hangings but also for the inventive soft toys or 'primeval creatures', as the students described them, which Bauhaus students sold to raise funds at the Weimar Christmas Fair.

The first textiles workshop Craft Master at Weimar was Helene Börner, who had taught at van de Velde's School of Arts and Crafts and generously allowed her students the use of her own looms, thus providing the weaving workshop with essential equipment still lacking in other workshops. On Helene Börner's arrival the shortlived 'Women's Department' of the *Vorkurs* seems to have been absorbed into the weaving workshop, which was regarded as a 'natural' female domain.

It was the weaving workshop's regeneration of a moribund craft which makes its work so important to twentieth-century design. In the later nineteenth century a major effort had been made by William Morris and the many women who worked with him to return to the forms and techniques of medieval tapestry. Morris despised Renaissance and later work as 'an upholsterer's tool' because it sought to reproduce the forms of pictorial representation and chiaroscuro (light and shade) of oil painting. After Morris, however, the revival of what he termed 'the noblest of the weaving arts' once again reverted to a literal transcription of easel painting. It is significant that it should be the teaching of such largely non-figurative painters as Itten, Klee and Muche which contributed to the Bauhaus' transformation of a major craft form. Klee's teaching of textiles fed back into his own work and is an important feature in the development of one of the key artists of the twentieth century.

The close links between the *Vorkurs* and the weaving workshop are perhaps more easily traced than those of any of the other workshops. The work done on the use of materials and color theory is particularly evident in the Weimar textiles. Some of the studies for the Use of Materials component of the Basic Course, with its emphasis on rich contrasts of texture, the studies from nature and the exercises on ornamental abstraction, provided particular inspiration for the textile workshop students. Muche's etching of 1922, *A Little Romantic Alphabet of Forms*, is an interesting example of such direct influence. Muche himself commented:

My alphabet of forms from abstract painting transformed itself into a fantasy which, in the hands of the weaving women, became tapestries, carpets and fabrics.

At Weimar, Muche and Paul Klee shared the texiles teaching for a period developing, among other things, the students' repertoire of forms learned on the *Vorkurs*. Klee's lectures on formal composition were illustrated with examples drawn from his own work, and his characteristic mixture of organic, geometric and fantasy forms can be traced in the development of his textile students' work. Unlike Muche, Klee found the craft of weaving a stimulus and compared it, according to accounts by his students, with the making of music which was of abiding interest throughout his life; he had been a musical prodigy and continued to play in music ensembles throughout his time at the Bauhaus, both at Weimar and Dessau. Klee's work with the textile students appears to have been of mutual benefit; forms drawn from weaving may be seen increasingly in his paintings of this period and such abstract fantasies undoubtedly influenced the students' textile compositions, for 'compositions' each of the early tapestries might fairly be called.

Anni Albers, who was a student in the weaving workshop from 1922, wrote of her fellow students:

They began amateurishly and playfully, but gradually something grew out of their play, which looked like a new and independent trend . . . unburdened by any practical consider-

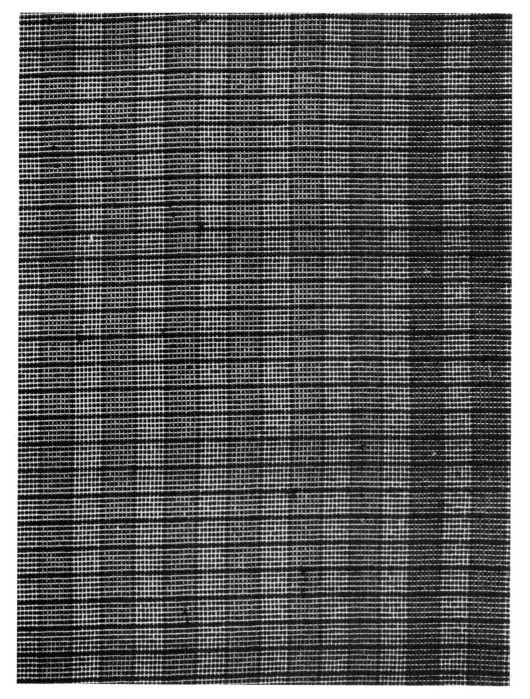

Below A rug or wallhanging by Margarete Leischner using strictly geometric forms drawn from the *Vorkurs*. Courtesy of Barry Friedmann Ltd.

Left Tapestry or cover woven by Gunta Stölzl in 1923 using white, black and gray threads with gold-colored metallic thread. Kunstsammlungen zu Weimar © DACS 1991.

ations, this play with material produced amazing results, textiles striking in their novelty, their fullness of color and texture and possessing often a quite barbaric beauty.

The most famous of all the Bauhaus textile designers, indeed arguably the most eminent and influential textile designer of her time, is Gunta Stölzl (1897-1983), who appears to have had a particular status in the weaving workshop from her arrival there in late 1919. Gunta Stölzl studied painting in Munich from 1914-19, serving as a Red Cross Nurse during the First World War. She came to the Bauhaus first as an apprentice in the mural painting workshop as soon as the School opened, quickly transferring to the weaving workshop, and was early marked out as one of its most promising students. In 1922, together with Benita Otte, Stölzl was

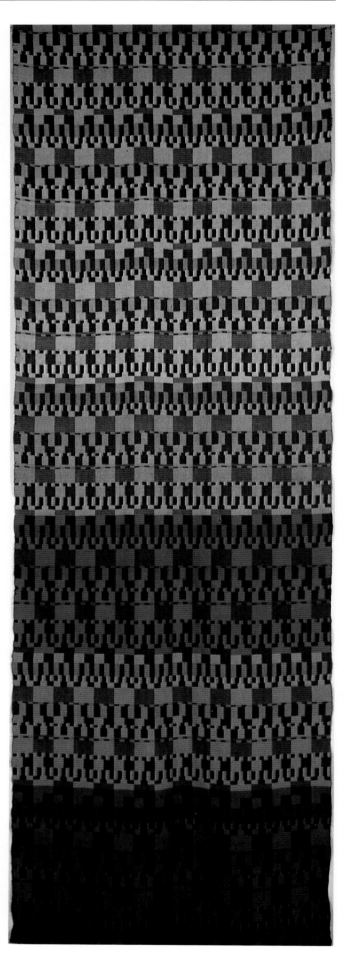

Above A tapestry using abstract forms by Helene Jungwick, 1921. Kunstsammlungen zu Weimar.

Far Right Textile designs by Agnes Roghé, 'Meterware', 1923/24. Kunstsammlungen zu Weimar. 'Meterware' was one of the earliest Bauhaus fabric designs to be sold by the yard.

Right Anni Albers' fabric samples, wool woven with cellophane and chenille. Bauhaus Archiv, Berlin. The weaving workshop at Dessau produced innovative designs using cellophane for its light-reflecting qualities for use as curtaining in large public buildings.

Right above Wallhanging by Benita Otte, showing Klee's influence in its subtle mixtures of forms. Kunstsammlungen zu Weimar.

Right below Wallhanging woven after a design by Paul Klee. Kunstsammlungen zu Weimar. Klee's work in the weaving workshop can be seen to have fed back into his painting from the Dessau period onwards.

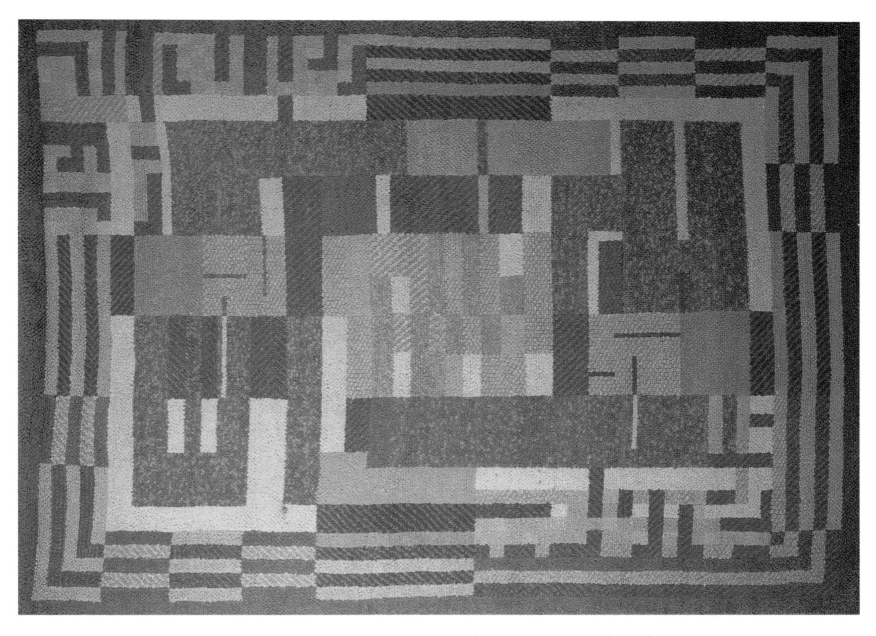

sent to Krefeld for advanced training courses in textiles and dyeing, and two years later Itten asked his former student to set up and run a weaving workshop at the Mazdaznan center in Herrilberg, Switzerland. When she returned to her work at the Bauhaus, her experience and flair made her the obvious candidate to take over the leadership of the workshop. Muche, however, who had always expressed his lack of interest in

the technical process of weaving, remained the nominal Master until his departure from Dessau to teach at Itten's school in 1926.

Stölzl then became workshop head until the dissolution of the Bauhaus in 1931, a key example of a Bauhaus Young Master, a former student trained in Bauhaus method who combined the role of teacher of form and teacher of craft. Stölzl had the added distinction of combining her work as workshop head and teacher with an extraordinary ability to design both one-off tapestries and serial productions. Her own distinctive textiles, together with her teaching and designs for industry, make her a key Bauhaus figure, and such was her influence that, in her own right, she is regarded as one of the leading textile designers of the twentieth century. Her recorded observations of the weaving workshops at Weimar and Dessau offer a unique and authoritative insight into the production process. She describes the qualities necessary for an apititude for textiles:

Love of the material, a feeling for the many, varied characteristics of the yarns, anticipatory imagination, a sure sense of color, patience, perseverance, ingenuity and nimbleness, both spiritual and manual, were the prerequisites of the work.

In 1931, the year of the Dessau Bauhaus' dissolution, Stölzl wrote in the Bauhaus magazine of the weaving workshop's:

Pictorial composition, surfaces that would bring a wall to life . . . For this creation, this transformation of experience, there was no pattern book from the past, no technical or intellectual recipe. With the new generation of Bauhaus painters, we were searching in the whirligig chaos of artistic values.

Stölzl's best known work, the richly colored and extravagantly patterned gobelin of 1926/27, now in the Bauhaus Archiv, Berlin, is a perfect example of bringing 'a wall to life'. It also has direct compositional links with Muche's etching *A Little Romantic Alphabet of Forms* and a comparison of the two is instructive. Stölzl was searching in her analysis of the work of this period:

Our textiles were still permitted then to be poems heavy with ideas, flowery embellishments and individual experience . . . they were the most easily understandable and, by virtue of their subject matter, the most ingratiating articles of those wildly revolutionary Bauhaus products. Gradually there was a shift . . . we made an effort to become simpler, to discipline our means and to achieve a greater unity between material and function.

'The greater unity of material and function' was an integral part of Gropius' policy shift towards 'Art and Technology: A New Unity', begun in Weimar but achieving its peak at Dessau. This shift is particularly clearly marked in the weaving workshop, especially as the technical resources at Dessau offered up-to-date equipment and conditions of work of a kind only to be dreamed of at Weimar. Single tapestries, as well as rugs and carpets, continued to be produced at Weimar by a succession of remarkable designers, Otti Berger, Anni Albers as well as Gunta Stölzl. The strength and inventiveness of the Bauhaus training can perhaps best be seen, however, in the way in which the 'weaving women', both staff and students, turned their energies to the production of designs for industry at Dessau, using innovative materials such as cellophane and

raffia, together with more conventional materials, in designs that could be produced by commercial machinery to be sold as 'yard goods'. As Stölzl herself defined the change in an article in 1926:

Today in all fields of design there is a quest for law and order. Thus we in the weaving workshop have also set ourselves the task of investigating the basic elements of our particular field. For example, while at the beginning of our Bauhaus work we started with image precepts – a fabric was, so to speak, a picture made of wool – today we know that a fabric is always an object of use . . .

The modern looms at Dessau were a vital factor in the change from exclusive one-off textile pieces, which Stölzl perceived by 1931 to be 'autocratic . . . the richness of color and form . . . did not integrate, it did not subordinate itself to the home'. The Jacquard loom, which combined the facility of weaving very complicated designs with comparative ease of operation, became especially important in the production of prototypes for industry. The multiplicity of prototypes produced for industrial production at the Bauhaus during the Dessau period were, in Stölzl's terms, 'clearly capable of serving the needs of the room and the problems of the home'. The process was aided by the fact that mechanical reproduction could be made to reproduce any handloom effect.

As became the practice with the metal workshop and its extremely fruitful partnership with such lighting manufacturers as Kandem, the weaving workshop forged extraordinarily successful links with industry. Study visits to and close working relations with such leading textile manufacturers as Polytextil-Gesellschaft (Polytex) of Berlin and Pausa of Stuttgart were an essential element in this partnership between art and industry. Polytex manufactured a range of textiles called the 'Bauhaus Collection', which were distinguished by their unobtrusive patterns and practicality. The designs of such 'weaving women' as Agnes Roghé, whose 'Meterware' was one of the Bauhaus' first designs to be sold by the meter; Otti Berger, whose distinguished work included both one-off designs and experimental designs made for industrial production; and Stölzl herself, who avidly spearheaded experimental work with such new materials as cellophane and 'artificial silk' (rayon) for machine production; met a particular need from progressive architects and interior designers working in both private and public spaces for functional, unobtrusive textiles appropriate to modern lifestyles.

The workshop was extraordinarily systematic in its approach to design, assessing not only the needs of commercial producers but also such problems as acoustic absorption, transparency and 'doublesidedness' – many of the fabrics were designed to have no front or back but to be attractive on each side. Designs for both home and public use were tested for washability.

The very restraint of such designs enhanced their usefulness and adaptability. Otti Berger and Gunta Stölzl, among others, incorporated cellophane into some of their materials for greater richness of effect and light-reflective quality, and some of these densely woven fabrics could be adapted for wallcoverings as well as used for drapery. Cellophane was also incorporated into the weave of drapery material commissioned from the workshop by the ADGB Labor Union

Opposite Advertising material for Bauhaus wallpapers designed in 1931 by Joost Schmidt. Bauhaus Archiv, Berlin. The rolls of wallpaper are shown unfurling, with the slogan 'The future belongs to Bauhaus wallpapers' reflected in a metallic or crystal ball.

Above and Below
Watercolor designs on graph paper by Gunta Stölzl for textiles to be woven on a jacquard loom. Courtesy of the Trustees of the Victoria and Albert Museum © DACS 1991.

Above Watercolor design for a carpet by Gunta Stölzl, 1928. Courtesy of the Trustees of the Victoria and Albert Museum © DACS 1991.

Right Stölzl's tapestry is one of the best known of all Bauhaus designs. Bauhaus Archiv, Berlin, © DACS 1991. Stölzl herself described the weaver's approach to such pieces as 'searching in the whirling chaos of artistic values . . . at the beginning of our Bauhaus work we started with image precepts – a fabric was, so to speak, a picture made of wool. Today we know that a fabric is always an object of use.'

Building at Bernau, near Berlin, and designed under Anni Albers' leadership. This material posed particular problems as it needed to be both light-reflective and able to absorb sound in such a reverberant interior. With the collaboration of the Zeiss-Ikon-Goetz factory, a glistening, cellophane-ribbed surface side was evolved, the woven cellophane enhancing the light-reflecting qualities of the material, while the back side used soft chenille to help absorb the sound.

The Bauhaus weavers thus addressed a central problem of the International Style public interior: that of reducing noise in large bare spaces constructed from concrete and plate glass, which have none of the sound-muffling qualities of traditional floor coverings and furniture, while still maintaining maximum light levels. The progress of the weaving workshop during the Weimar and Dessau periods clearly demonstrates the decisive shift between the early 'Expressionist Bauhaus' and the realization of Gropius' vision of a 'new unity of art and industry'.

Graphic Work at the Bauhaus

Left Herbert Bayer, cover design for the Bauhaus Journal (1928). Bauhaus Archiv, Berlin, © DACS 1991. This makes brilliant use of the journal itself as the background to its own cover design, together with the designer's tools of set-square and pencil, and the irreducible solids of sphere, cone and cube.

From the very beginnings of the Bauhaus, with Lyonel Feininger's 1919 woodcut title page *Cathedral* for Gropius' *Manifesto*, so evocative of the utopian socialism of the years following the First World War and the perfect visual equivalent to Gropius' stirring words, graphics were an integral part of the Bauhaus. By its very nature, graphic design in the widest sense became one of the most familiar forms of Bauhaus activity. From the designs for the Bauhaus signets, through advertising, typography and exhibition design, as well as the Bauhaus books, what might be called Bauhaus house style was radical, distinctive and enormously influential on all aspects of modern graphic design.

The Weimar Bauhaus inherited the printing presses and bookbinding equipment of the former School of Arts and Crafts. The presses were used for printing outside work and were thus a valuable means of providing much-needed income in the early years. The workshop, under the direction of Craft Master Carl Zaubitzer, was equipped with the means to produce lithographic prints, etchings and woodcuts which offered valuable training to the apprentices. Apart from the routine commissions of the early years, the workshop produced between 1921 and 1924 a prestigious series of ten large portfolios of graphic work,

New European Graphics. This was announced in the prospectus of 1921 in the following terms:

For the first time we offer the collector the chance to purchase an international collection of graphic works, which in the current economic situation is otherwise impossible to obtain. The collection is of fundamental importance as a representation of the most significant artists of Germany, France, Holland and Russia.

Gropius hoped that the portfolios would be a source of income for the Bauhaus and used his international contacts to obtain gifts of original drawings from as wide a range of artists as possible, urging them to contribute to:

A document which will demonstrate how the artistic generation of our times shares the ideas of the Bauhaus and is willing to make sacrifices.

It was clear by 1921 that the Bauhaus had to initiate such outside work in order to ensure the viability of the School, although in the event only two of the ten portfolios were printed as advertised by 1922, with two others following by 1924. Although these represent the most important venture of original printmaking by avant-garde artists in the Germany of this period, raging inflation in the years of publication meant that even the costs of production were not covered, and by the end of 1923, when the currency was stabilized, there was no market for such splendid collectors' items. However the two first portfolios, devoted to works by Bauhaus Masters and *German Graphics*, are landmark collections of early twentieth-century printmaking.

Lyonel Feininger (1871-1956), first Master of Form of the printing workshop, contributed the title page, cover and list of contents and two of the fourteen prints. The other pairs of prints were by Itten, Marcks, Schlemmer, Klee, Muche and Lothar Schreyer, another member of the *Sturm* circle who had been appointed to run the theater workshop in 1921. The *Masters' Portfolio* (published in an edition of 110) attracted a great deal of attention throughout Europe and provided the means for close collaboration between the seven Masters and the workshop apprentices. The range of prints is wide in technique and subject matter, ranging from Itten's lithograph *The House of the White Man*, a utopian architectural construction, to Gerhard Marcks' woodcut *The Owl*, which demonstrates his continuing interest in the medieval German woodblock tradition and makes for an interesting comparison with the work he was currently doing as Form Master in the ceramics workshop. There were also color lithographs, including Klee's witty *Hoffmanesque Scene*, printed in black, yellow and violet and Schreyer's color design for his own drama, *Kindersterben* (Child Dying).

The participation of the seven Masters is an interesting testimony to the fact that at Weimar the workshop facilities were not restricted to those formally assigned to them. There was an informal arrangement by which anyone, staff and students alike, could make use of technical expertise and equipment in any workshop; there are various accounts of students otherwise unconnected with the weaving workshop, for example, wandering in to use the looms. This freedom, which disappeared in the tighter structures of the Dessau Bauhaus, helps to explain the fact that so many *Bauhaüsler* produced work of extraordinary versatility.

Below Paul Klee *Hoffmanesque Scene* 1921, oil on canvas. Courtesy of the Trustees of the British Museum. Klee was a much-loved teacher at the Bauhaus and his work there from 1920 had a decisive effect on his painting as, in order to teach, he had to analyse his own creative process. He later published some of his theoretical writings and teaching notebooks as *Pedagogic Notebooks*, which are still in print today.

The *Masters' Portfolio* is wholly representative of the graphics of the early years at Weimar – even Feininger's title page shows the free-form lettering widely used in these years of the so-called Expressionist Bauhaus.

Other collector's editions were produced at the Bauhaus at this time, including *Utopia* and limited editions of print collections by single Bauhaus Masters including Feininger, Marcks and Kandinsky. The apprentices were also engaged in more repetitive tasks which helped Bauhaus funds, such as the printing of business stationery and work for the Weimar government. In 1923, Bauhaus student Herbert Bayer was commissioned to design a set of banknotes for the Thuringian government, designs of elegant simplicity that denote the worthlessness of the currency they represent; the mark was being catastrophically devalued even as the notes were being printed in huge denominations of up to 2 billion marks.

In the printing workshop, working relations between Feininger, the Master of Form and his Craft Master Carl Zaubitzer were cordial, although Zaubitzer was a craftsman of the old school. Paul Klee, Form Master of the bookbinding workshop, was not so fortunate in his Craft Master colleague, Otto Dorfner, who was also a designer and owned the affiliated bookbindery which had originated in the Weimar Arts and Crafts School. The day-to-day working of the bookbindery proved so difficult that the contract with Dorfner and the workshop was canceled by the Bauhaus in 1922, although Dorfner continued to provide bindings for such portfolios as *New European Graphics*.

The watershed of the Bauhaus' development, the 1923 exhibition, galvanized the printing workshop into producing new ideas; the publicity for the exhibition and the inaugural Bauhaus Week began a full six months before the event and the workshop's resources

were put under strain. A series of 20 postcards were produced by Masters and students to publicize the exhibition, and show the huge variety of graphic styles currently in use at the Bauhaus, including the free expression of the individual students' ideas encouraged on the *Vorkurs*. The highly personal 'map' of Weimar by the student Kurt Schmidt is an example of this free expression of ideas. The map includes not only the tourist landmarks of Goethe's house and Liszt's house, but also such Bauhaus landmarks as Itten's workshop, all drawn to a subject scale of Schmidt's own devising.

The publicity material for the exhibition as a whole, however, revealed the extent to which the Bauhaus was indebted to the European avant-garde of the time. The asymmetrical influence of De Stijl in particular was reinforced in the graphic work of this period by the presence of Theo van Doesburg and his lectures on De Stijl in Weimar. Russian Constructivism also had an influence on Bauhaus graphics, as did the bizarre juxtapositions seen in the paintings and collages of Dada and Surrealist artists.

It was Moholy-Nagy, however, who had no formal connection with the printing workshop, who had the greatest direct influence on the new generation of graphic designers. Moholy, with his intense interest in all forms of visual communication, film, photography, photomontage and print, was convinced of the power

Above Oskar Schlemmer, cover design for *Utopia: Documents of Reality*, 1921. Kunstsammlungen zu Weimar © The Oskar Schlemmer Family Estate. The painterly, Itten-inspired free style of the lettering is characteristic of the approach to typography prevalent at Weimar at the time.

Left Kurt Schmidt, Bauhaus postcard 19, 1923. Bauhaus Archiv, Berlin. Kurt Schmidt's offering to the set of 20 Bauhaus postcards designed for the 1923 Exhibition shows a subjective student view of the historic city of Weimar with Itten's studio, 'the Temple' included alongside the Goethe and Liszt Houses.

Above Lyonel Feininger's woodcut *Figures on the Shore* from *New European Graphics*, 1921. Bauhaus Archiv, Berlin © COSMOPRESS Geneva and DACS London 1991.

Right The title page of the same portfolio. Bauhaus Archiv, Berlin © COSMOPRESS Geneva and DACS London 1991. Both graphics show Feininger's unique and inimitable style.

of what he termed 'visual-typographical' design to reflect and influence changes in society.

The fact is that form, size, color and arrangement of the typographical materials contain a strong visual impact. The organization of these possible visual effects gives a visual validity to the content of the message as well, this means that by means of printing the content also being defined pictorially . . . (this is) the essential task of visual-typographical design.

Moholy designed advance publicity for the Bauhaus Books as well as co-editing, with Gropius, the fourteen volumes, which were to appear between 1925 and 1934. Moholy was also responsible for the design of the jackets of the hardback editions and most of the paperback covers and the typographical layout of the series in general — a considerable undertaking given his teaching and other commitments. The titles included key works by Bauhaus masters such as Klee's *Pedagogical Sketchbook* (1925), Kandinsky's *Point and Line to Plane* (1926), as well as Gropius' *Bauhaus Buildings in Dessau* (1930) and Moholy's own *Painting, Photography, Film* (1925). The books, which were a vital part of the Bauhaus' relationship with the wider world, were marked by their use of Moholy's radical fusion of typographic, graphic and photographic elements. Particularly influential was Moholy's use of asymmetry, bold type and 'point and line to plane' (irreducible geometric shapes in graphic terms, including arrows).

In the workshop's first major Bauhaus publication of this genre, *The State Bauhaus in Weimar 1919-23*, the catalogue of the 1923 exhibition, Moholy declared his overriding aim in the use of typography in the following terms, 'type is an instrument of communication. It has to be clear communication in its most penetrating form.'

The exhibition catalogue, with an unusual square format, was designed by Herbert Bayer (1900-85), a Bauhaus student from 1921, who was to become one of the most radical and influential of the Young Masters when he was appointed head of what was to become known as the graphics workshop at the Dessau Bauhaus. Bayer, like Marianne Brandt, was typical of the versatile Bauhaus student become Young Master. He specialized in all forms of graphic design, from advertising material to typography and exhibition design. His most extraordinary work at this time must be the designs for the newspaper and cigarette street kiosks projected in 1924. These designs make dramatic use of bold blocks of color and signify their function in 'the most penetrating form', in Moholy's terms. The giant chimney of the cigarette kiosk was intended to emit puffs of smoke to reinforce its message.

Bayer considered himself 'primarily a painter . . . painting is the continuous link connecting the various facets of my work'. He trained first in the Bauhaus mural painting workshop and his work owed much to the influence of Klee and Kandinsky's teaching, particularly in respect of aspects of analytical drawing and the elements of visual perception. His work also demonstrates the key shift between the quintessential Weimar printing workshop production, the collector's *New European Graphics* and Dessau's emphasis on commercial design in the renamed Graphics Department which addressed Gropius' policy shift toward 'Art and Technology: A New Unity'. The technology in this case was linked to current developments in the German printing industry, which included the introduction of the German Industrial Standard paper sizes (DIN) in 1922. Bayer limited the typefaces he used to sans serif, to avoid any association with handwritten characters.

In 1925 Bayer produced his first designs for a universal sans serif typeface, using only structurally essential parts of each letter and limiting the forms to an irreducible series of arcs and straight lines. Bayer's 'Universal Type' was not cast as a typeface and was used mainly for advertising display. However his principles of 'clarity, precision and abstract form' were to prove both influential and controversial. His desire to eliminate capital letters (at this time all nouns in German were set in upper case) in the interests of economy as well as logic caused particular controversy. As Bayer himself phrased it:

We do not speak with a capital 'A' and a small 'a' to convey one sound, we do not need large *and* small letter symbols. One sound, one symbol.

However critics of the Bauhaus sans-serif lower case faces were incensed by the fact that the majority of Bauhaus staff insisted on its use in articles written by them in books and periodicals, and it has never become widely acceptable for large blocks of type in such contexts. Bayer's catalogue design and typography for The Bauhaus: Fifty Years Exhibition of 1968 is disconcerting to read for those accustomed to conventional print. The internationalism of lower-case sans-serif typefaces particularly enraged extreme Nationalist opinion in Germany – the National Socialists employed Gothic typefaces as a potent signifier of their ideology.

The typographical workshop's contribution to the design of posters and advertising and display material of infinite variety made a huge impact, however. Used in combination with graphics or with photographic blocks, as in Moholy and Bayer's joint design for the cover of the 1928 *Bauhaus* magazine, the witty fusion of complex elements became a classic of twentieth-century graphic design.

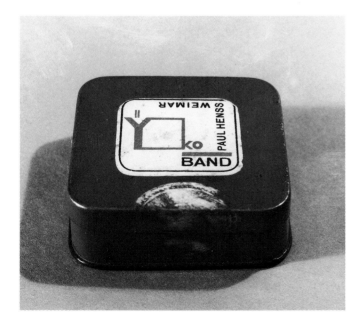

Metallwerkstatt

gesch.
Höhe ca. 35 cm
AUSFÜHRUNG
Kristallspiegel-Glasplatte, Felsenglasrohr, Glasschirm, Zugfassung

ME 1

TISCHLAMPE AUS GLAS
VORTEILE
1 beste Lichtzerstreuung (genau erprobt)
2 sehr gefällige Form
3 besonders schönes Licht
4 praktisch für Schreibtisch, Nachttisch usw.
5 Glocke festgeschraubt bleibt in jeder Lage unbeweglich

Left Herbert Bayer, page from the Bauhaus catalogue of 1925 showing the Wagenfeld-Jucker glass and metal table lamp. Bauhaus Archiv, Berlin © DACS 1991. Bayer's radical and highly influential typography and layout are seen in their most characteristic form.

Below left Joost Schmidt, typewriter ribbon tin design, 1924/25. Bauhaus Archiv, Berlin. Schmidt also designed the publicity material for the Weimar company of Paul Heuss.

Below Herbert Bayer, page from the Bauhaus catalogue of 1925 showing the Wagenfeld-Jucker lamp in a different form with a metal base. Bauhaus Archiv, Berlin © DACS 1991.

Metallwerkstatt

gesch.
Höhe ca. 35 cm
AUSFÜHRUNG
Messing vernickelt, Glasschirm, Zugfassung

ME 2

TISCHLAMPE AUS METALL
VORTEILE
1 beste Lichtzerstreuung (genau erprobt) mit Jenaer Schottglas
2 sehr stabil
3 einfachste, gefällige Form
4 praktisch für Schreibtisch, Nachttisch usw.
5 Glocke festgeschraubt, bleibt in jeder Lage unbeweglich

Joost Schmidt (1893-1948), one of the most versatile and popular of the Young Masters, moved from his post as head of the sculpture workshop to take over as head of the graphics workshop on Bayer's departure in 1928. Schmidt (or Schmidtchen as he was universally and affectionately known) trained as a painter before being wounded and captured in the First World War. He joined the sculpture workshop at the Bauhaus when it opened and as a student he worked on the Sommerfeld House. To earn some money as a student Schmidt helped Otto Dorfner, who ran his own business as well as being Craft Master of the Bauhaus bookbindery. Schmidt, who was six feet tall despite his affectionate diminutive nickname, taught himself the complex gold-leaf lettering needed for the parchment certificates Dorfner commissioned from him by borrowing, in the words of his widow Helene Schmidt-Nonné, 'some of those beautifully decorated medieval books from the Weimar State Library and diligently copying the script during his spare time at home'. Schmidt's poster for the 1923 exhibition, which so wittily incorporates Schlem-

mer's redesigned Bauhaus signet in its dynamic diagonal, is one of the Bauhaus' best known and most influential designs.

By 1928, when Schmidt became Master of the graphics workshop, advertising had become such an important feature of Bauhaus work that the department went through another change of title as an indication of its changed function. The department, which had begun

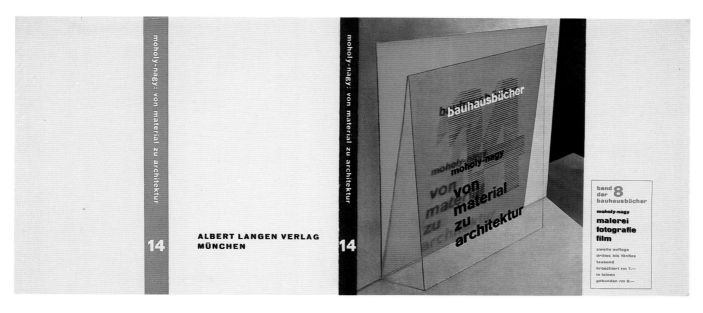

as the printing workshop under Feininger and Zaubitzer, and was then the graphics workshop under Bayer, became the advertising department under Schmidt. His design brochures for the Dessau tourist office in 1930 made striking use of photography and photomontage, juxtaposing Dessau's most famous product, the Junkers airplane, against elements of classical architecture to signify the city's past and present. Schmidt designed both graphic display material and advertising display stands which communicated Bauhaus ideas to a large and varied public. Advertising material for Bauhaus wallpapers, for example, made simple, witty and dramatic use of graphics and photomontage.

Schmidt's advertising department team broke new ground in exhibition design, using graphics and photographic material to convey clear and concise information to the public. The complexity of such operations can perhaps be judged by the theme for the Junkers stand at the Gas and Water Exhibition in Berlin in 1929, which was entitled 'Idea-Form-Purpose-Time'. The design for the stand was so advanced that, on seeing his firm's gas appliances installed ready for use in the

Bauhaus setting, Professor Junkers realized how relatively old-fashioned the technical design of the equipment was. 'Something has to be done for these appliances', he is reported to have exclaimed, 'they don't fit in here!' The designs were modified immediately and changed soon after.

Bauhaus exhibition design was on show throughout Europe until this dimension of the Modern Movement, among others, was crushed by the Nazis. However it remains a lesser known aspect of the Bauhaus style which reached a public untapped by other forms of Bauhaus activity, and set a display style in both Europe and America for a considerable period. The gulf between the utopian socialism of the early Bauhaus and the 'Unity of Art and Industry' may be seen as particularly deep in Bauhaus graphics. After Gropius' departure in 1928, the talents of the renamed advertising department was increasingly put at the service of industrial capitalism.

The Furniture Workshop

Left Marcel Breuer's design
for the B5 side chair was
manufactured by Standard
Möbel, Berlin from 1926 and
quickly became one of the
company's best-selling items.
Bauhaus Archiv, Berlin.

Furniture derived from Bauhaus designs may now be seen in public and private spaces throughout the world: over 60 years after the first designs were manufactured, chrome and leather chairs based on Bauhaus prototypes still signify modernity. The origins of such radical designs were in the cabinet-making workshop of the Bauhaus at Weimar. The wood workshop taught quite distinct skills and was discontinued after 1925, achieving its most important work in the 1923 Sommerfeld House, where students like Marcel Breuer and Joost Schmidt, later to become Young Masters in different spheres of design, produced their first commissioned work. Schmidt's carved decorations (since destroyed) are interesting both in themselves and in relation to his later well known graphic designs. His carving employs an eclectic mixture of symbolic references to Sommerfeld's ship-building interests and to contemporary painting and sculpture styles such as Futurism. Breuer's block-like wood and leather chairs, an important stage in his development, show the influence of another contemporary art movement, Constructivism.

The cabinet-making workshop, to which Breuer was apprenticed, was set up only in 1921 with Gropius himself as first Form Master, although as he was so often busy elsewhere, Itten took on much of his teaching in addition to his own work on the Basic Course. The workshop, like others at Weimar, was not well equipped and wood was in very short supply. Students were trained in the key techniques of furniture-making but the design emphasis was on a radical rethinking of all current domestic furniture forms, a rejection of most traditional middle-class furniture types — the heavy bedroom and living room 'suite' of matching furniture, for example, and a complete rejection of all forms of ornament and decoration.

The desire to go back to first principles in seating had some curious consequences, of which Breuer's so-called African chair is perhaps the best known. As was concurrent practice in the pottery workshop, a return to basic principles was conceived in terms of a return to primitive forms, and the African chair is perhaps best understood in relation to some of Marcks' and Krehan's earliest decorated pots. The chair might more properly be called a ritual throne and used an amalgam of forms derived from African and Magyar sources (Breuer was Hungarian) to form a bizarre and exotic seat; an extraordinary debut from Breuer, whose famous tubular steel and leather chairs were to follow only four years later.

Breuer's furniture designs for the Sommerfeld House of the same year are also dramatic, even aggressive, but in an entirely different style. The seating units and tables appear from photographs to have been monumentally block-like and immovable, with no hint of the 'transparency' and lightness he was soon to consider so vital. They were constructed in cherrywood and black leather, with curious cut-away geometric profiles to the chairs and five-legged table designed for the entrance hall of the villa.

The cabinet-making workshop derived its forms from a variety of sources, despite its avowed rejection of all previous prototypes. The influence of William Morris' Sussex chairs of the 1860s (in themselves a reworking of English folk forms) was strong at Weimar, together with Morris' overall design ethos of 'form follows function' which informed so much Bauhaus de-

Right A page of photographs from *Bauhaus Journal No I* of 1926, illustrating Marcel Breuer's chair designs, beginning at the top with the Africa chair. The caption to the photographic sequence reads 'Every day we are getting better and better . . . in the end we will be sitting on resilient columns of air.' Bauhaus Archiv, Berlin.

Left Two versions of Marcel Breuer's Lattenstuhl (slat chair) of 1922. Bauhaus Archiv, Berlin. Another version with a woven striped seat appears third from the top in the illustration from the *Bauhaus Journal* opposite.

sign. The contemporary influence of Constructivism with its ideas of multi-functionality, together with the mass-produced bentwood chairs produced by Thonet, were also important.

Strongest of all, however, was the influence of De Stijl and Gerrit Rietveld's Red-Blue chair in particular, the single most influential source for Bauhaus chair design. The Red-Blue chair was designed 1917-18, first published in *De Stijl*, No 11 in September 1919, and in its famous colored form in 1923. However its importance for the Bauhaus workshop lay in its form; the chair is strictly functional and its elements are separated into 'sticks' and 'planes', soon to be further accentuated by the use of bright, primary De Stijl color. This clear and overt expression of structure was a decisive influence on Bauhaus furniture design. Breuer's slatted chair design, the Lattenstuhl of 1922, for example, the focus of much attention at the 1923 exhibition, is obviously derived from the Red-Blue chair. It was made of cherrywood (although pearwood versions exist) with seat and back strapping woven in the textiles workshop. A similar Rietveld-like separation of elements can be seen in Erich Dieckmann's cherrywood and cane sidechair of 1922 and matching armchair of 1925.

As was the case with other aspects of Bauhaus design, the cabinet-making workshop was galvanized by the 1923 exhibition. Workshop production was stepped up to provide sets of furniture for the experimental Haus am Horn. Breuer produced furniture for the dining room, and Dieckmann's designs were used for the woman's bedroom, while other designers provided furniture for the nursery and kitchen, these last proving particularly successful. The last years at Weimar were especially busy. Although links with industry were not

formed by this stage, there was constant demand for the products of the workshop, which by this time included toys as well as painted furniture. Breuer designed a set of painted nursery furniture which was light and functional and became very popular. The workshop went into serial production to make sets of

Below Erich Dieckmann's round table (diameter 104cm) of 1925 is carved from mahogany and cherry wood. Bauhaus Archiv, Berlin.

Right Gerrit Rietveld's well-known Red-Blue chair was designed in 1918. Stedelijk Museum, Amsterdam © DACS 1991. It had a vital influence on Bauhaus chair design, as can be seen when it is compared with Marcel Breuer's Lattenstuhl on the previous page.

Below Lily Graf's carved wooden chest of 1921 shows the influence of Itten's Basic Course, particularly in its use of contrasting textures. Bauhaus Archiv, Berlin.

scaled-down furniture for children's homes and kindergartens. The success of the nursery furniture is partly attributable to the ways in which it responded to contemporary theories of childcare, especially to such factors as hygiene and the importance of primary colors in early learning experience.

Alma Büscher, the only woman working in the workshop, also designed sets of brightly colored wood toys that could be taken apart and put together to form a variety of ships and other simple forms. She wrote of her work on children's designs, 'Work and play are interchangeable, as at the Bauhaus'. Consequently her brightly colored, scaled-down unit furniture was designed to be taken apart as a series of boxes, to be played with as well as used for storage purposes.

The introduction at Weimar of what was termed 'combination' furniture also addressed a contemporary problem, that of lack of space in the domestic interior. This approach can be seen at its simplest in the Haus am Horn kitchen, where cupboard and shelf units are combined with hygienic work surfaces to form what might fairly be called the first fitted kitchen. Free-standing units which combined various functions in other rooms of the house were also designed at this time. Breuer designed a unit for the dining room of the Haus am Horn which combined glass-fronted display cabinets with storage cupboards and open shelving. Gropius himself designed the furniture for his office in 1923. The cherrywood desk had a built-in paper rack which was cantilevered, as were the arms of the matching upholstered chair.

Such combination furniture designed for multifunctional use was influenced by Russian Constructivism, especially by the work of Alexander Rodchenko who taught at the Moscow equivalent of the Bauhaus, the Vkhutemas. Rodchenko's 1924 design, produced in collaboration with his students, for a metal-frame and wood collapsible desk which combined a drawing-board function with a surface for dining and writing in an ingenious folding form is a *tour de force* of the combination genre. A more traditional form of combination work unit is Bengt von Rosen's secretaire of 1923-24. This is made from light cherrywood and darker plumwood and combines drawers and cupboard units with a fold-down writing surface. From a later period, but still reflecting the Weimar aesthetic of fine wood craftsmanship, is the grandly architectural

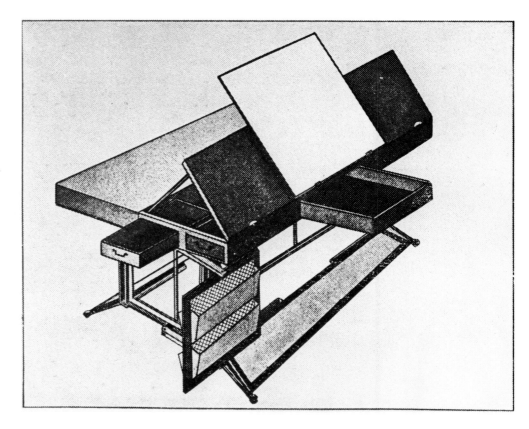

Above Combined drawing/writing and dining table designed in Alexander Rodchenko's studio at Vkhutemas in 1927. Museum of Modern Art, Oxford © Rodchenko Family Estate. Constructivist designs such as this were a decisive influence on Bauhaus combination furniture.

Left Cherrywood dining table designed by Marcel Breuer in 1924; the tapestry is by Gunta Stölzl. Kunst-sammlungen zu Weimar.

department until the last years of its existence, the influence of architectural design was paramount in many of the workshops.

With the move to Dessau, Breuer became one of the newly appointed Young Masters. He remained as head of the newly designated furniture workshop until 1928 when Albers took his place. Breuer's radical use of tubular steel in the making of furniture necessitated a change of name for the workshop, as cabinet-making implied working with wood. Breuer rejected all tradition. In 1927 he wrote, 'Our work is unrelenting and unretrospective; it despises tradition and established custom'. The idea of using lightweight tubular steel rather than wood (which was by its very nature traditional) in chair design, occurred to Breuer as he cycled around Dessau on his newly acquired Adler bicycle. So impressed was he by the potential suggested by the strength and lightness of the tubular steel construction, particularly by its curved handlebars, that he approached the manufacturers with the idea of adapting the material for furniture construction. Adler rejected the idea and so Breuer purchased the preformed steel from the bicycle manufacturer's suppliers and welded the prototype Wassily chair himself, with the help of a local craftsman.

I took the pipe dimensions (approximately 20mm in diameter) from my own bicycle . . . I didn't know where else to get it or how to work it out.

Breuer dubbed the design the Wassily chair because Kandinsky was so enthusiastic about it, and ordered

Above Sideboard, made from cherry wood with black linoleum top, 1930, an example of combination furniture produced in the latter years of the Bauhaus. Bauhaus Archiv, Berlin.

walnut combination wardrobe storage unit designed by Lily Reich at Dessau in 1930-33 when she was head of the workshop, which by then had become the interior design department. Like much Bauhaus combination furniture, its solidly architectural character reinforces the fact that, although the Bauhaus had no architecture

Left Marcel Breuer designed the B33 sidechair in 1927/28. Bauhaus Archiv, Berlin. It is one of the most familiar of all Bauhaus furniture designs and is still used today all over the world.

several for his house. This first design proved too heavy and Breuer continued to work on it, although he was unable to patent it, as a photograph of the chair in a Dessau newspaper which aroused great interest technically constituted 'publication' in German law, which forbids the patenting of published designs.

Breuer was encouraged, if surprised, by the interest in his design. In 1927 he wrote:

... When I saw the finished version of my first steel club armchair, I thought that this out of all my work would bring me the most criticism. It is my most extreme work both in its outward appearance and the use of materials, it is the least artistic, the most logical, the least 'cosy' and the most mechanical.

He might have added that it was also the most democratic; its bicycle origins carry over the associations of that most democratic means of transport into another everyday functional object. The chair, together with others designed by Breuer, was produced by Standard Möbel in 1926 and by Thonet (who took over Standard Möbel in 1929) in 1931. Thonet had long been famous throughout the world as the hugely successful manufacturer of bentwood chairs. The designs were cheap,

easily assembled, light and elegant: the firm's most popular design, No 14, sold around 50 million copies worldwide between 1859 and 1910. By the 1920s, Thonet were still producing new designs for mass production and were among the first to commission designs using steel. Indeed Breuer's designs may be said to echo Thonet's success with bentwood, notably in terms of standardization of parts, economy in mass production, movability and what Breuer termed 'anonymity'. The design of the cantilevered metal chair was not Breuer's invention, despite his close association with it, but that of the Dutch designer Mart Stam.

In 1928 an advertisement for a Breuer-designed range of seating types manufactured by Standard Möbel, called 'Breuer Metallmöbel', staked considerable claims for the furniture types:

Tubular steel furniture with fabric seat, back and armrests is as comfortable as well upholstered furniture, without having its weight, price, unwieldiness and insanitary quality ... all types can be taken apart. The parts are interchangeable.

The simple 'B' chairs of metal and fabric became one of the great industrial successes of the Bauhaus, used in

Far left Marcel Breuer's designs for nursery furniture of 1923 were very popular. Kunstsammlungen zu Weimar. They were made in a variety of sizes of plywood painted in bright colors.

Right Marcel Breuer designed the tubular steel Wassily chair in 1925. Courtesy of the Trustees of the Victoria and Albert Museum, London. It is so called because Kandinsky admired it so much that he insisted on its inclusion among the furnishings of his master's house at Dessau.

the Bauhaus' own buildings and still familiar today throughout the world. As was the case with the Bauhaus metal light fittings, the design of the chairs transposed what had always been regarded as an industrial material, in this case chromed steel, into a domestic context. The possession of such furniture quickly became a potent signifier of the owner's modernity — indeed this is still the case two generations later. The timeless quality of the chairs contributes to their popularity as classics of modern design. True cult status for the chair as a work of art, rather than as a mass-produced object familiar to all, however, is reserved for the chair designs of the architect Mies van der Rohe. So exciting were the applications of the new technology that chair design became the focus of a great deal of attention at the Bauhaus: with the use of mold-breaking new materials and all traditional associations stripped away, the chair could be seen as a species of art-object, combining beauty and utility. The converse of this, in the period of the directorship of Hannes Meyer, was to turn production over to the design of minimal furniture for workers' housing.

Breuer's cantilevered metal chairs were designed for mass production, whereas Mies' Weissenhof and Barcelona designs were luxury objects. The Weissen-

hof arm and side chair designs of 1927 were made of cantilevered nickel-plated tubular steel and woven cane. Both chairs were designed for the Weissenhof estate, near Stuttgart, a showpiece for the 1927 German Werkbund Exhibition, built under Mies' direction and with contributions from all the key architects of the day, Gropius and Le Corbusier among them. Mies' interest was not in compactness and mass production, but in minimal sculptural elegance and comfort: the chair design exploits the springiness of the metal and the balance of the curves is reminiscent of much contemporary sculpture — Brancusi's bronzes, for example. The chair is still in production, together with the leather-upholstered Barcelona chair: both are now cult objects of twentieth-century design.

The Barcelona chair was designed for Mies' German Pavilion at the 1929 World's Fair in Barcelona, a key structure of twentieth-century Modernism and one which first drew public attention to Mies' importance and uniqueness as an architect. The Pavilion was openplan and the use of precious materials, Roman travertine, onyx, polished steel and etched green and smoked glass, all contributed to the jewel-like spatial effect. The chairs were conceived as part of this composition and designed to occupy fixed, throne-like positions. They were made from chromium-plated steel strips and the finest black leather upholstery, supported on rubber webbing. Steel strip, unlike steel tubing, is a material that demands hand welding to form such elements as the leg joins in the Barcelona style, a highly skilled operation impossible in mass production. Such a luxurious object is also very heavy and more or less immobile, the very antithesis of Breuer's ideal of 'transparency', lightness and movability.

During Hannes Meyer's Directorship of the Bauhaus, from 1928 to 1930, the furniture workshop was amalgamated with the metal and mural painting workshop to become the Department for Interior Design, first under the leadership of Albers and then under Alfred Arndt, from 1929 to 1932. Attention was turned to space-saving, minimalist, multi-purpose furniture for workers' dwellings and much use was made of plywood in conjunction with metal. Low-cost furniture was designed for the Bauhaus People's Dwelling exhibited in Leipzig in 1929. Much ingenuity was displayed in the design of the folding furniture, particularly that of chairs and beds. The workshop patented a metal and wood workchair in 1931 with a seat that locked into place when weight was applied. Meyer despised what he perceived as the elitism of Breuer's design aesthetic and demanded collectivism in workshop design. It is indeed ironic that designs derived from both Breuer's and Mies' originals should be both ubiquitous and popular today, whereas the designs produced in Meyer's workshops are much less widely known.

Above Unlike Breuer's designs, Mies van der Rohe's Barcelona chair, first designed for Mies' German Pavilion at the 1929 World's Fair in Barcelona, was not designed for mass-production. The Barcelona chair, still widely used today, is a luxury object, designed for elegance and comfort. Courtesy of the Trustees of the Victoria and Albert Museum.

Left As with the Barcelona chair, Mies' Weissenhof chair is elegant and sculptural. The Weissenhof chair exploits the springiness of the metal. Both chairs have become cult objects of Bauhaus design. Courtesy of the Trustees of the Victoria and Albert Museum.

DIE OPER

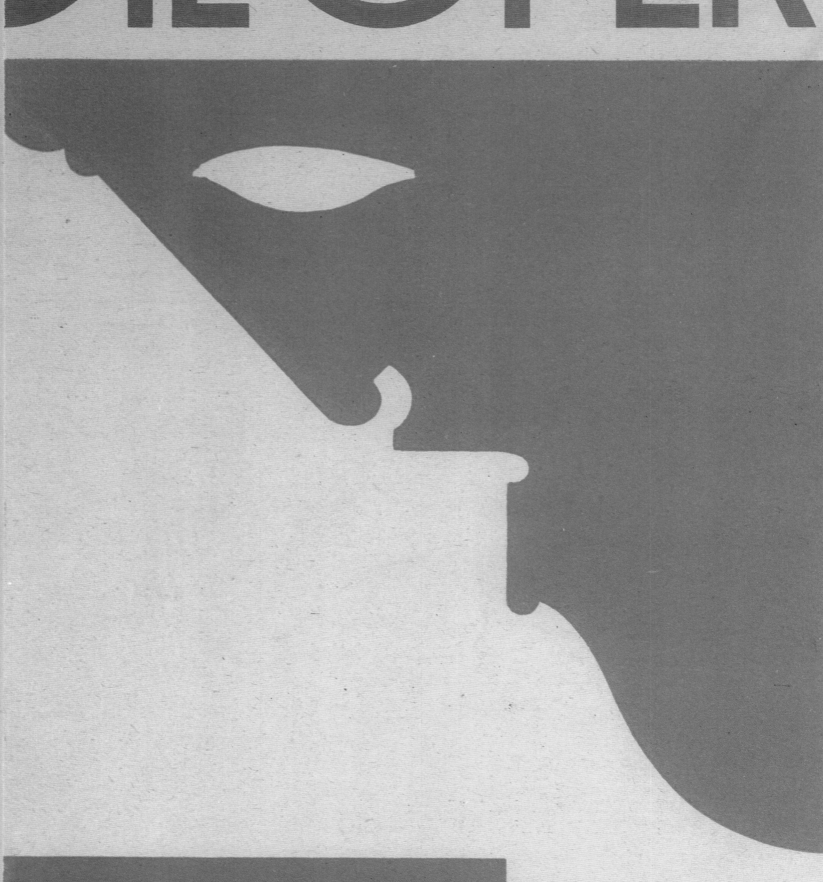

BLÄTTER DES BRESLAUER STADTTHEATERS

Theater at the Bauhaus

Theater, in its widest sense, had always been part of Bauhaus life from the earliest days at Weimar. The improvised and often eccentric dress of some of the students made them a public spectacle around the city, while the Bauhaus Jazz Band achieved a more welcome public acclaim. The festivals that marked the seasons of the year — the Festival of Lanterns for Gropius' birthday, Midsummer Eve, the Festival of Kites (or Dragan Festival) and Christmas — were all celebrated with elaborate ritual and were essentially public occasions. The Festival of Kites was especially useful as a public relations exercise, a foretaste of the touring productions which were later to make the Bauhaus Theater famous throughout Germany. Tut Schlemmer recalled that the kites were:

Fantastic creations that sometimes were so beautiful they could not even fly. They were however proudly carried through the city, thus reconciling some of the angry citizens and making them our friends.

All the Bauhaus workshops were primarily concerned with public rather than private art and there can

be no art by its very nature more public than that of theater, except perhaps the primary discipline of the Bauhaus, architecture. As in the making of a building, theater requires the close collaboration of a team of craftspeople trained in different skills, all working to the same end. The workshop provided an essential focus for the exploration of one of the most important issues in the development of the Bauhaus, that of space and the human form's relationship to it, but it also provided an arena for contained creativity and a formal means of expressing the music, dance and the love of parody that were so marked a feature of Bauhaus life at Weimar. Oskar Schlemmer, whose work as director of the stage workshop made it famous throughout Europe, wrote in 1926 of the development of theater at Weimar.

The stage was there on the very first day the Bauhaus opened, because enjoyment in designing was there on that very first day. This enjoyment was first expressed in the celebrations . . ., in the invention of masks, the making of costumes, and

the decoration of rooms. And it was expressed in *dancing, dancing, dancing!* The music evolved from the Bauhaus dance, which developed from the clown dance into the 'Step'; from the concertina to the jazz band. From this 'dance for everyone' evolved the 'dance for the individual' and its reflected form on the stage: the chromatic-normal, the mechanized ballet. From inspiration, whim, and a mind to do something primitive, evolved *parodies* on existing theater, opera, drama, circus, and variety shows . . . We are breaking conventions where they seem to be already shaky, and we are experimenting with creating new forms.

The theater workshop was started in 1921 with Lothar Schreyer (1886-1966) as its first Master. Schreyer initially trained as a lawyer before deciding on painting and the theater as a career. He joined the *Sturm* circle in 1916 and helped found its Expressionist drama school, of which he was director from 1918-20 at the same time as running an experimental theater in Hamburg. It was in Hamburg that Gropius first saw his work and persuaded him to join the Bauhaus in 1921. Schreyer's avant-garde theory of theater aimed to create, in his own words 'a single organism in which word, sound color and movement were united'.

Schreyer's mystical presentations were recorded in a graphic notation of his own invention, with a series of symbols which fixed on the page the actor's precise body movements, together with his or her voice rhythms, pitch and volume. Schreyer's tenure at the Bauhaus ended when staff and students alike fiercely criticized the rehearsal of his own presentation *Moonplay* for performance at the 1923 exhibition.

Schreyer's critics found his work obscure and incomprehensible and Gropius was persuaded to concede to the weight of Bauhaus opinion. The 1921 color design from the stage presentation *Kindersterben* (Child Dying) gives some idea of Schreyer's productions.

Kindersterben was one of a group of three dramas first performed at Schreyer's avant-garde theater in Hamburg and was, like the others, produced as a modern Mystery play. The actors were elaborately costumed and heavily masked, their words intoned to the accompaniment, in the case of *Kindersterben*, of a glass harmonica and a gong, all combined to achieve in Schreyer's words 'an overwhelmingly powerful transcendental effect'. Schreyer designed several painted figures as the visually dramatic center of the performance. As he described them, 'Each of these figures was a non-objective, sculptural, colored work of art'. The color design was one of the pair Schreyer contributed

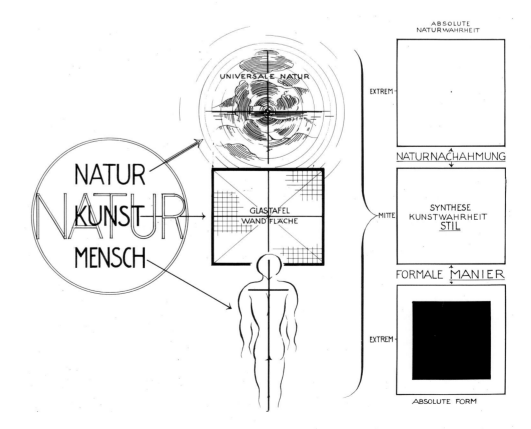

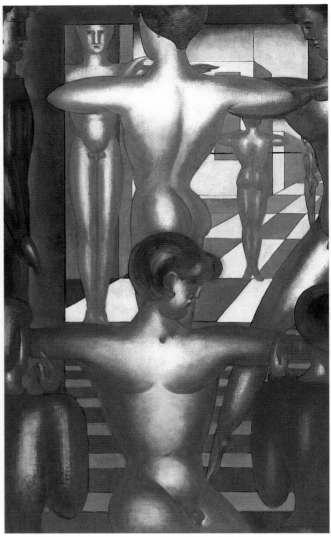

to the first Bauhaus Portfolio and may well be one of Schreyer's structural designs for such figures.

After Schreyer's departure, Oskar Schlemmer was persuaded to step sideways from his primary position as Master of Form in the sculpture workshop; he also

taught in the mural painting workshop, and some life drawing too at this time. Schlemmer (1888-1943) was born in Stuttgart and in 1906 became a student of Adolf Hoelzel, who was to be a major influence on Schlemmer as he had been to Itten. In 1910 in Berlin Schlemmer began his work with avant-garde theater and dance, and after being wounded in the First World War he began working on the *Triadic Ballet*, his most famous work, which was to occupy him for many years to come. While experimenting with theater and dance he continued his development as a painter both of easel painting and of murals, exhibiting at the *Sturm* gallery and reaching his mature style by about 1919. Earlier, he had made an important contribution to the mural decoration of the main building of the Werkbund Exhibition in Cologne in 1914, where his work first came to Gropius' attention. He was invited to join the Bauhaus staff in December 1920, but was at first distinctly reluctant, particularly as there was no stage. At this time he wrote that:

The future development of the Bauhaus stage lies in darkness. The Bauhaus lacks the first prerequisite: the stage, and Gropius ignores all suggestions to this effect.

Schlemmer kept up his working relationship with the Stuttgart Theater, where he was working as a designer, while he was teaching at the Bauhaus in the first years. It was at Stuttgart that the full version of the *Triadic Ballet* was first performed, with music by Paul Hindemith, in 1923. Meanwhile at the Bauhaus Schlemmer's dynamic leadership of the theater workshop, which spilled over into other aspects of Bauhaus life, made him one of the most influential figures there. Schlemmer remained at the Bauhaus until 1929 when he resigned over the new Director, Hannes Meyer's, attempt to politicize the workshop. After his departure the workshop was closed and only informal experiments survived.

At Weimar Schlemmer taught life drawing and directed the sculpture and mural painting workshop. He contributed significant murals to the entrance hall of the Bauhaus building for the 1923 exhibition, later obliterated at the instigation of the National Socialist Director of the Weimar Academy of Art which took over the building after the departure for Dessau. At Dessau Schlemmer had the means to continue his work in experimental theater, with a purpose-built stage space. He was also active outside the stage workshop, particularly with his coursework on 'Man' in 1928-29. Schlemmer's versatility was extraordinary even for a Bauhaus Master, but his painting is a constant touchstone throughout his career and the sense of the body in space in his paintings is that of a painter who was also a sculptor, dancer and choreographer. In Schlemmer's words:

The human figure, plucked out of the mass and placed in the separate realm of the stage [or, it follows, the painting] is surrounded by an aura of magic and thus becomes what one might call a space-bewitched being.

Schlemmer's best known painting, *Bauhaus Stairway*, was made in 1932 in Breslau, where he received the news of the final closure of the Bauhaus in Dessau by the Nazis. During the next eleven years (he was to die in 1943), Schlemmer was denied by the Nazis the means of exhibiting his work, teaching, or having his works performed: some of his finest paintings were included in the notorious 'Degenerate Art' exhibition in Munich in 1937. In 1939 he worked fulltime camouflaging public buildings. In 1940 he joined other refugee artists, including former Bauhaus colleagues Gerhard Marcks and Georg Muche, at an experimental paint laboratory at Wuppertal.

Left Oskar Schlemmer's painting *Bauhaus Stairway* was one of several versions of the subject painted in 1932 in Breslau after the closure of the Bauhaus. Hamburg Kunsthalle © The Oskar Schlemmer Family Estate.

Below left Oskar Schlemmer's color lithograph poster for performances of the *Triadic Ballet* in 1924. © Oskar Schlemmer Theater Estate.

Below right Schlemmer's color designs for mural paintings for the workshop at the Weimar Bauhaus. © Oskar Schlemmer Family Estate. These were executed for the Bauhaus Exhibition in 1923, obliterated by the Nazis and have recently undergone a programme of restoration.

In *Bauhaus Stairway*, what might be called Schlemmer's triadic principle can be seen in the group of three central figures ascending the central staircase of the Dessau building, so familiar from contemporary photographs, and a key architectural element together with the great glass wall behind it. The clear, symbolic transparency of the building and the upward move-

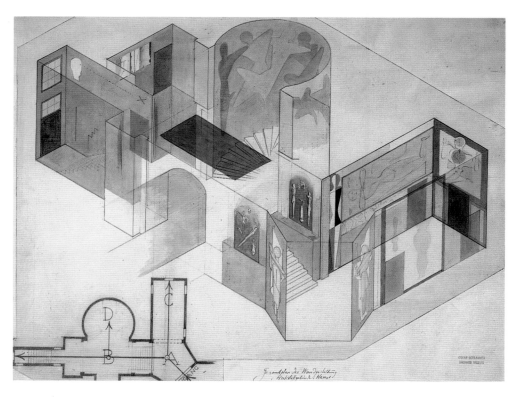

Right The gold sphere, one of the figures in Oskar Schlemmer's *Triadic Ballet*. This photograph was taken at a performance in 1922. © Oskar Schlemmer Theater Estate.

Below A photograph by T Lux Feininger of the Bauhaus Band in 1928. Bauhaus Archiv, Berlin. Oskar Schlemmer can just be seen at the top, with, below, Werner Jackson, Xanti Schawinsky, Hermann Röseler.

ment of the youthful figures seem to echo the hope for the future expressed in Gropius' speech in the happier days of the opening of the building in 1926, when Gropius conceived the Bauhaus as a:

Spiritual center . . . for our young people, the creatively talented young people who some day will mold the face of our new world.

In his painting, his stage work and his teaching, Schlemmer posed the question:

What does the artist do? He makes the unclear appear clear, the unconscious conscious, the impossible possible: plucks the one out of the chaos. Simplicity out of multiplicity.

Schlemmer was to develop these ideas in his course on 'Man' at Dessau in 1928, in which his well known drawing *Man in the Sphere of Ideas* was first used. He aimed at nothing less than the total regeneration of theater and saw what he termed 'the theatrical dance' as becoming the starting point for such a regeneration.

Unencumbered by tradition, the dance is independent and predestined to drive gently into the senses whatever is new.

In the fourth of the Bauhaus Books, *Die Bühne im Bauhaus* (The Bauhaus Stage) of 1925, Schlemmer distinguished the general sense of theater as:

The entire realm lying between religious cult and naive popular entertainment. Neither of these things, however, is really the same thing as stage. Stage is *representation* abstracted from the natural and directing its effect at the human being.

Schlemmer, who abhorred the traditional proscenium arch and had an adaptable form of stage designed for him by Gropius at Dessau, writes of theater space in the following vivid terms:

This confrontation of passive spectator and animate actor preconditions also the form of the stage, at its most monumental as the antique arena and at its most primitive the scaffold in the market place.

The central figure of Schlemmer's stage is 'Man the Dancer' (*Tanzermensch*).

He obeys the law of the body as well as the law of space: he follows his sense of himself as well as his sense of embracing space . . . the *Tanzermensch* is the medium of transition into the great world of the theater.

Schlemmer sought a synthesis of the abstract and rational with the organic and emotional. The metamorphosis of man the dancer into man the art figure was to be achieved without loss of man's centrality or humanity. For Schlemmer man is the measure of all things. However bizarre the costumes, there is always an underlying human dimension in Schlemmer's work — often an engaging element of self-parody.

Apart from the human dancers, Schlemmer's Bauhaus stage was to accommodate inanimate figures on a relative scale, which could be huge to emphasize their importance or marionette-size to stress their insignificance. The inanimate figure had been advocated by the English stage reformer, Edward Gordon Craig, who coined the term *Ubermarionette* (super-marionette) to describe it.

Schlemmer published his working drawing for *The Two Solemn Tragedians* to accompany his essay on 'Man and Art Figure' in *The Bauhaus Stage* in 1925. The mechanized figures, mounted on wagons, in the drawing are huge, fully the height of a proscenium arch on a traditional stage. Their 'voices' were amplified by megaphones proportionate to the size of the figure and there was sometimes an orchestral accompaniment. The figures personified 'lofty concepts such as Power and Courage, Truth and Beauty, Law and Freedom'. Their arms were hinged to make possible 'sparse and significant gestures'. In contrast to these columnar and helmeted giants 'there is natural man with his natural voice, moving about in the three zones of the stage . . . establishing the dimensions vocally and physically'. Such ideas, particularly that of the giant inanimate figure and the marionette, have recently been revived to spectacular effect in avant-garde theater and musical productions, especially on the English stage.

Schlemmer's theories and the workshop's various skills were employed in his best known work *Triadic Ballet*, first performed in its entirety in 1922 in the Stutt-gart Landestheater, and in the following year at the Bauhaus week in the Nationaltheater, Weimar. The three parts of the *Triadic Ballet* formed a 'structure of stylized dance scenes', according to Schlemmer 'developing from the humorous to the serious'. Twelve roles were danced by two male and one female dancer in extraordinary costumes constructed of padded cloth and stiff papier mâché forms coated with metallic or colored paint. The three ballets were:

First a gay burlesque, with lemon yellow drop curtains. The second, ceremonious and solemn, is on a rose colored stage. And the third is a mystical fantasy on a black stage.

The *Triadic Ballet* was originally set to a score constructed of selections from the work of classical composers, but in 1926 Paul Hindemith composed a new score for mechanical organ or player piano, an appropriate non-human accompaniment. The *Triadic Ballet*, from which all Schlemmer's later stage work developed, achieved the integration of dance and music with body decoration and sculpture and the fusion of space and form, light and color, sound and movement. This seminal work became the precursor of much modern and post-modern dance in many important respects, especially in the United States, where interest in Schlemmer has resulted in reconstructions of his work in essential 'black box spaces' in such dance venues as New York's The Kitchen in 1982 and the Solomon R Guggenheim Museum in 1984.

At Weimar, the workshop productions were performed on what Schlemmer termed 'a sort of dubious suburban podium' (of the Weimar theater) but at Dessau Gropius designed a 72-meter-square adjustable double-sided platform which opened both to the Bauhaus main hall, with its rows of Breuer-designed seating, and the canteen. Gropius further developed his architectural ideas on theater with his design for the Total Theatre for Erwin Piscator in Berlin in 1926. This

Below Ludwig Hirschfield Mack: varied sequences from a projected colored reflected light composition, *Cross Composition*, devised and performed about 1923. The forms were achieved by moving the colored templates used in the projection. Bauhaus Archiv, Berlin.

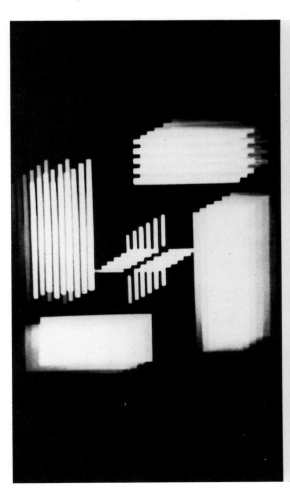 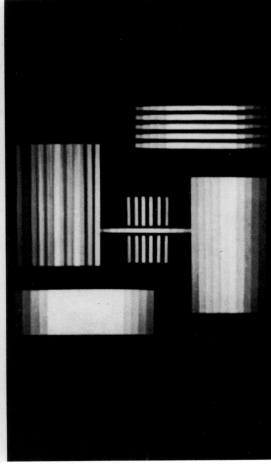 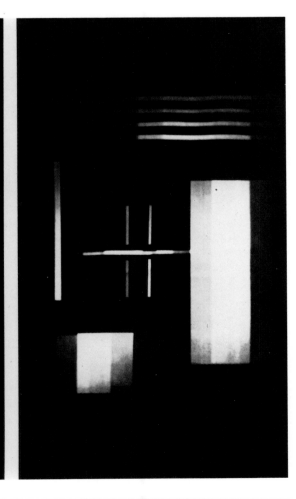

Right Xanti Schawinsky *Bauhaus Versuchscomedia* (Bauhaus Experimental Comedy), mixed media using photographic material by Lux Feininger, 1927. Bauhaus Archiv, Berlin. Interesting comparisons may be made with Irene Bayer's photograph of the theater workshop, taken in the same year, page 149.

Below Oskar Schlemmer's costume designs for *The Triadic Ballet*, c.1922. Mixed media — ink, gouache, metallic powder, graphite and collage. The Busch-Reisinger Museum, Harvard University © The Oskar Schlemmer Theater Estate.

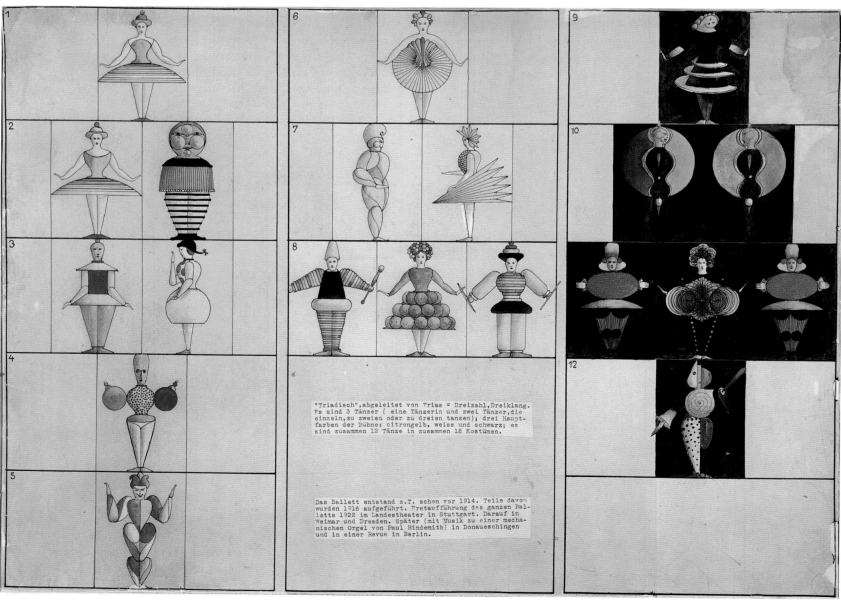

"Triadisch", abgeleitet von Trias = Dreizahl, Dreiklang. Es sind 3 Tänzer (eine Tänzerin und zwei Tänzer, die einzeln, zu zweien oder zu dreien tanzen); drei Hauptfarben der Bühne: citrongelb, weiss und schwarz; es sind zusammen 12 Tänze in zusammen 18 Kostümen.

Das Ballett entstand z.T. schon vor 1914. Teile davon wurden 1916 aufgeführt. Uraufführung des ganzen Balletts 1922 im Landestheater in Stuttgart. Darauf in Weimar und Dresden. Später (mit Musik zu einer mechanischen Orgel von Paul Hindemith) in Donaueschingen und in einer Revue in Berlin.

was a revolutionary design intended, in Gropius' words, to accommodate:

The new interpretation of theatrical space ... to create a great and flexible instrument which can respond in terms of light and space to every requirement of the theatrical producer.

Work on the theater was abandoned when Hitler came to power.

The stage workshop, according to its prospectus of 1926-27, offered training for:

Painters and technicians, actors, dancers and stage directors in practical and theoretical collaboration for the common objective of the new stage form.

Tuition was offered in stage design, which included the making of masks and costumes, movement and dance, stage direction and the technical skills of both front and back stage. Schlemmer and Xanti Schawinsky, one of the students, collaborated on a series of dances entitled Gesture Dances, which Schlemmer also performed in at Dessau. The dancers wore full-face masks and their costumes of red, blue and yellow were heavily padded with wadding. Schlemmer described the effect of the tights and masks as 'to regroup the various and diffuse parts of the human body into a simple, unified form'.

Moholy-Nagy and Kandinsky were also involved in the theater at the Bauhaus. Moholy contributed an essay to The Bauhaus Stage entitled 'Theater, Circus, Variety', in which he outlined his theory of the Theatre of Totality. This was to do away with the 'peep-show' concept of the proscenium arch and engage:

The multifarious complexities of light, space, plane, form, motion, sound, man – and with all the possibilities for varying and combining these elements – (into) an ORGANISM.

Above Heinz Loew, mechanical stage models, from a reconstruction made in 1967/68. Bauhaus Archiv, Berlin.

Left Oskar Schlemmer's design for 'The Abstract' from The Triadic Ballet of 1922 from a reconstruction of 1985. © The Oskar Schlemmer Theater Estate.

Below left Oskar Schlemmer Man in the Sphere of Ideas, from Schlemmer's course 'Man', taught at the Bauhaus, Dessau in 1928, ink, pencil and colored pencil on paper, mounted on board. © The Oskar Schlemmer Family Estate.

Below Wassily Kandinsky: stage design for Mussorgsky's Pictures from an Exhibition – the great Gate of Kiev. Kandinsky directed a production to his own design in 1929 at the Friedrich Theater in Dessau. Cologne Institute for Theatrical Studies © ADAGP Paris and DACS London 1991.

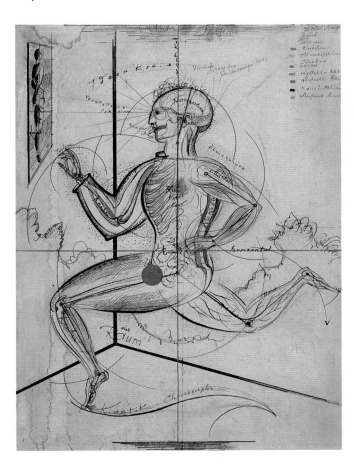

Bauhaus toys, the spinning toys which demonstrated color mixtures, produced a light show with projected abstract shapes moving to music: a synthesis of light, color and sound. Work pioneered in this field at the Bauhaus has its modern counterpart in a wide range of cultural activity from modern dance to rock spectaculars such as those designed by Jean Michel Jarre. In a different mode, Kandinsky designed a staging of Mussorgsky's orchestral *Pictures from an Exhibition*, which he also directed at the Dessau Theater in 1929, the year of Schlemmer's resignation and the closing of the theater workshop.

The Bauhaus presentations were toured extensively and were important in establishing good public relations between the Bauhaus and the outside world, as the Festivals had done in the early days at Weimar. The Bauhaus Jazz Band, which played only improvised music, not exclusively jazz, also toured extensively and was famous even in Weimar Berlin. Many of the Band's members were theater workshop students, the soprano and alto saxophone player was Xanti Schawinsky, who contributed to the Bauhaus stage as a designer and acted as Schlemmer's assistant. After the dissolution of the Bauhaus, Schawinsky was invited by Josef Albers in 1936 to join the teaching team (which included Anni Albers) at Black Mountain College, North Carolina. Schawinsky taught painting and experimental theater, later publishing his theories as *Play, Life, Illusion*. The presence of such key Bauhaus figures at Black Mountain College was an important channel for disseminating Bauhaus ideas in the United States. Merce Cunningham, generally regarded as the father of high modernism in American dance, and the painter Robert Rauschenberg were both at Black Mountain at this time.

At Dessau the Jazz Band provided music for the famous Bauhaus parties, which were always thematic and masterminded by Schlemmer and the theater workshop. Schawinsky recalls the feverish preparation that went into the Beard, Nose and Heart Party of 1927. He was put in charge of decorations; Herbert Bayer designed the invitations:

A costume advisory office was opened in Berlin . . . the *Bauhaüsler* helped all they could . . . heaps of hair were turned into wigs, whiskers in every style . . . noses molded, according to the injustice of nature, hearts invented . . . afterward everyone said it was the handsomest festival ever mounted in Berlin.

Two years later, the Metallic Festival was mounted at Dessau. A newspaper report of February 12 1929 described the slide which had been constructed between the two Bauhaus buildings:

Even the most dignified personalities could be seen sliding down into the main rooms . . . every area of the populace was represented. Most of them in 'metallic' costumes.

Musical accompaniment was provided by three bands, and a whole variety of metal instruments including tinkling bells. The newspaper account concluded:

The party sparkled and shone and yet was of such friendly gaiety and merriment, without ever getting out of hand in any way, that all participants enjoyed it thoroughly.

It is small wonder that many *Bauhaüsler* memories of their student days recall the parties more vividly than their studies.

Moholy put his ideas into practice in 1929, with a production of Offenbach's fantasy opera *The Tales of Hoffmann* in which one of the tales is of a mechanical doll brought to life. The conservative world of opera did not take kindly to his radical ideas, although work by Moholy has since been influential in theater.

Work by the student Ludwig Hirschfeld-Mack bearing obvious relation to Moholy's work with light, particularly the Light-Space Modulator, such as *Reflected Light Composition* has also been influential in the theater and in rock music spectacles. Hirschfeld-Mack, who designed some of the most popular of all

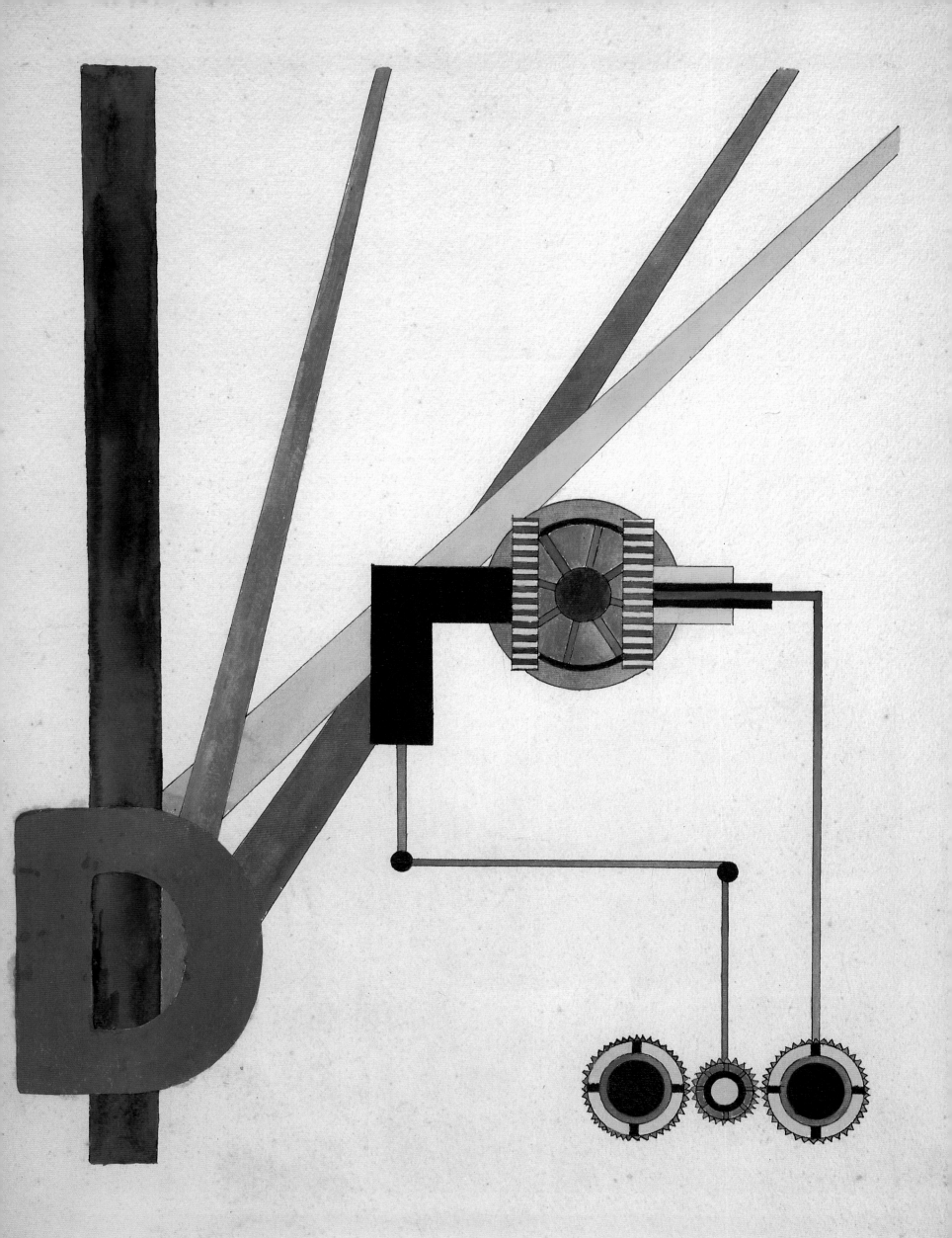

The Bauhaus After Gropius

Left László Moholy-Nagy
Composition c.1921.
Goauche and collage.
University of East Anglia
collection. Moholy here uses
collage as a tribute to the
dedicatee, the collage artist,
Hannah Hoch.

In 1926, Gropius wrote a broadsheet *Dessau Bauhaus: Principles of Bauhaus Production*. In it he described the Bauhaus workshops as:

Essentially laboratories in which prototypes suitable for mass production and typical of their time are developed with care and constantly improved. In these laboratories the Bauhaus intends to train an entirely new kind of collaborator for industry and the crafts who has an equal command of technology and design.

At the time he wrote this, however, there was no 'laboratory' for architecture – it was eight years before one was introduced. This seems ironic given the stress on architecture in the 1919 *Manifesto* – 'the ultimate aim of all creative activity is the building'. In the early years Gropius considered that intending architects should not receive a narrowly specialist training but that architectural skills should rest on a foundation of craft and design skills and theoretical work of the kind taught in the workshops and the preliminary course. Meanwhile key architectural projects such as the Bauhaus buildings at Dessau and the Masters' houses were designed by Gropius' own practice.

In the Dessau buildings, however, the space originally designed for Gropius' private architectural practice and used as such in the first years became the Bauhaus' own architectural department after two

Right Lux Feininger's 'Bauhaüsler' photographed around 1928. Bauhaus Archiv, Berlin.

Below Hannes Meyer and Hans Wittwer's projected design for the League of Nations building in Geneva, 1926/27. Bauhaus Archiv, Berlin.

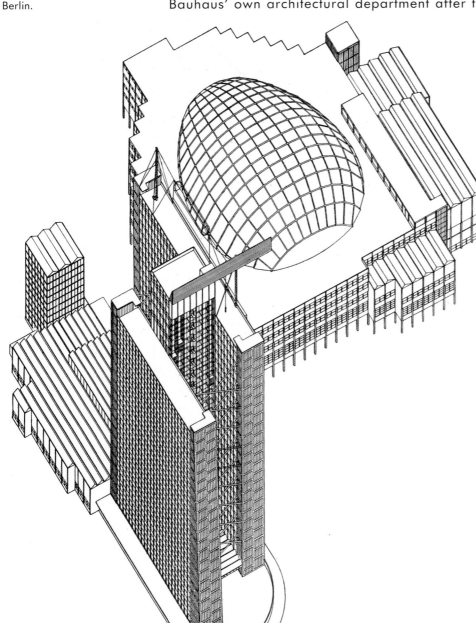

years, opening in 1927. The department had the same status as the workshops and could be proceeded to immediately after the preliminary course without any training in craft. Gropius appointed the Swiss architect Hannes Meyer (1899-1954), the architecture department's first Professor. Meyer had studied building in Basle and Berlin and town planning between 1909 and 1912 at the Technical University in Berlin. His interest in town planning led him to England to study the housing built for Cadbury's chocolate factory employees at Bournville and the housing development for workers at Lord Lever's soap product factories at Port Sunlight. While in England he also studied, as he later wrote, the country's 'social structures, the co-operative movement, theaters, cinemas and music halls', as well as the development of garden cities such as Letchworth. After service in the First World War, Meyer assisted in the design of the garden city for Krupps workers, the 'Margaretenhöhe' at Essen and set up in practice on his own account in Switzerland.

The initial work of the new architectural department under Meyer's direction was to assist Gropius in the completion of the experimental Torten estate, already discussed in the chapter on architecture at Dessau. The workers' estate, commissioned by the City of Dessau, was built in three stages between 1926 and 1928. On-site construction of standardized parts resulted in the basic building of each unit being completed in three days.

When Meyer joined the Bauhaus staff as Professor of the new architecture department early in 1927, he was highly critical of the Bauhaus as he found it and, in view of this and his known left-wing political opinions, it is not at all clear why Gropius, with all his experience of the power of right-wing opposition in the last years at Weimar, asked Meyer to head the new department. Meyer's decision to join the Bauhaus is perhaps even more difficult to understand in view of his openly stated views on architecture. Writing in *The Bauhaus Journal* of 1928, he began an article on his beliefs with a statement which challenged the very basis of Bauhaus belief:

All things in this world are a product of the formula: function × economy. All these things are, therefore, not works of art: all art is composition and, hence, is unsuited to achieve goals. All life is function and therefore unartistic.

Meyer concluded his polemic with the ringing words, 'Building is nothing but organization, social, technical, economical, psychological organization.'

Among the Bauhaus staff, old and new Masters alike, Meyer's views caused much dissension. His views on art alone were sufficient to guarantee that he would not fit easily into a teaching team which included such painters as Klee, Kandinsky and Muche – even Moholy insisted on the primacy of creativity, despite his passion for technological innovation. Meyer's emphasis on collective endeavor and the need for specialization was anathema to Breuer and Bayer, who resigned in 1928. Muche had resigned the previous year to join Itten's teaching staff. Moholy's resignation came in January 1928. Unlike his colleagues, who gave as reason for leaving the pressure of outside work, Moholy made his reasons for leaving perfectly clear in a letter to the Governing Body of the Bauhaus. He cites the growing specialization of the school:

As soon as creating an object becomes a speciality, and work becomes trade, the process of education loses all vitality. . . . The spirit of construction for which I and others gave all we had – and gave it gladly – has been replaced by a tendency toward application. My realm was the construction of school and man.

A year after Meyer's appointment, Gropius resigned as Director of the Bauhaus, proposing Meyer as his successor. Gropius' contract had two years to run and the reasons for his leaving are still not entirely clear,

Above Heinz Loew's dramatic photograph of 1927/28, *Self Portrait with Shadowprofile*. Bauhaus Archiv, Berlin.

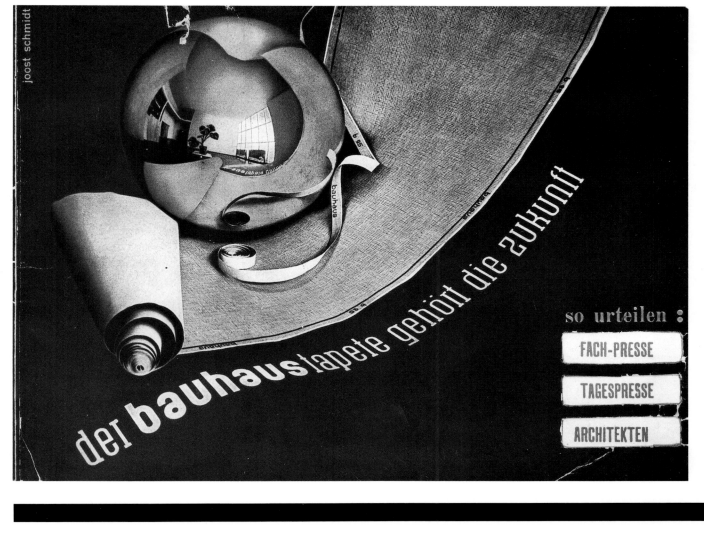

Left Joost Schmidt's striking and influential advertising material for Bauhaus wallpapers. The slogan reads 'the future belongs to Bauhaus wallpapers'. Bauhaus Archiv, Berlin.

12 gropius bauhaus bauten dessau

band der 1 bauhausbücher

gropius: internationale architektur

sechste auflage
broschiert rm 5
in leinen
gebunden rm 7

ALBERT LANGEN VERLAG / MÜNCHEN

Below Iwao Yamawaki's memorable photo-collage *The End of the Bauhaus* was first published in a Japanese journal in 1932. Bauhaus Archiv, Berlin.

although right-wing victories in recent elections must have been a factor in his decision. His letter of resignation to the Magistracy of the City of Dessau of February 1928 offers the following explanation for his decision to leave:

I would like from now on to be able to work and develop free from the restriction of official duties and responsibilities especially as my public commitments outside Dessau are steadily increasing.

Gropius' resignation and the naming of his successor created shockwaves throughout the Bauhaus. Gropius' address to the students provoked an emotional reaction. One of the student representatives, Fritz Kuhr, replied to Gropius' speech in terms that convey something of the atmosphere of the occasion:

For the sake of an idea we have starved here in Dessau. You cannot leave now. If you do, the way will be opened for the reactionaries. Hannes Meyer may be quite a fine fellow. I don't want to say anything against him. But Hannes Meyer as the Director of the Bauhaus is a catastrophe.

In reply, Gropius explained that in his time as Director:

90% of my efforts were expended defensively . . . Today the Bauhaus is one of the leading members of the 'modern movement', and I can serve the cause far better if I continue working in another part of the movement.

Meyer was able to restructure the courses after the departure of Gropius and such powerful Masters as Moholy, Bayer and Breuer. The architecture department became central to the work of the School. Several new teaching staff of international repute were appointed including, as a visiting tutor, the Dutch architect Mart Stam, the inventor of the tubular steel chair form, who had, it appears, been Gropius' first choice as his successor. The School now began an analytical and systematic research programme into architecture and design which affected all departments: furniture students, for example, were to research the number of clothes people of different income groups were likely to possess before designing wardrobes.

The teaching programme was also systematized. Activity in the School was rationalized into just four departments, architecture, advertising (which now took in the former print and graphic workshops, together with the newly formed photography workshop), the textile department and the department of interior design. This last incorporated the former metal workshop, the furniture workshop and the wall-painting workshop. For the first time in the history of the Bauhaus, formal instruction in painting was also given. This had the effect of marginalizing painting, removing it from its position at the very heart of the school's activities where it had been from the beginning with the appointments of the first Masters of Form at Weimar. The rationalization of the workshops, however, and their greater productivity, combined with the economic revival in Germany of 1927, brought in increased capital for the Bauhaus, which paradoxically now came nearer to achieving Gropius' original dream of self-sufficiency than it had ever done.

The interior design department under Alfred Arndt, a former student, made a substantial contribution to this, notably the royalties from a range of Bauhaus wallpapers made by Rasch Brothers. Meyer wrote that in 1929, the year of their introduction, 'more than 20,000 rooms in Germany and adjoining countries were papered with them'. The success of the unobtrusively designed range, which included washable wallpapers, was aided by a particularly dynamic campaign designed by the advertising department under Joost Schmidt. Meyer was to claim that 'annual production' at the School 'amounting to about RM 128,000 has been almost doubled . . . in the last business year' (he was writing in 1930) 'RM 32,000 has been paid out to students in wages and has enabled less wealthy students to study'.

All was not well at the Bauhaus, however, and several of the remaining staff from the old system expressed the desire to leave. Schlemmer explained the situation as he perceived it in March 1929:

All in all it seems that my time at the Bauhaus has ended. I want to leave. People – the students, me, too – are dissatisfied with Hannes because of his rough manner and lack of tact. The atmosphere at the school is not good. Bad enough that the entire Bauhaus question will soon be debated in the State Parliament.

Schlemmer was to leave a few months later, and the theater workshop was closed.

During the summer vacation of 1930 Meyer was dismissed on political grounds with three years of his contract still to run and without notice. He had never made any secret of his political beliefs, and in an angry open letter to Mayor Hesse which he published in the magazine *Das Tagebuch* on August 16 1930, he protested that he had been:

Stabbed in the back . . . My repeated assurances that I had never been a member of any political party remained futile . . . the Bauhaus cabal rejoiced. The local Dessau press fell into a moral derilium.

Meyer took the opportunity fiercely to denigrate the Bauhaus as he found it when he first arrived:

A Bauhaus whose potential exceeded its reputation by orders of magnitude, and which had been receiving an unprecedented amount of publicity . . . Inbred theories blocked every means of designing in a way that was right for living: the cube was king – its faces were yellow, red, blue, white, gray, black. This Bauhaus cube was given to children to play with and to the Bauhaus snob as a knick-knack . . . One ate and slept on the colored geometry which was the furniture. One lived in the colored sculptured forms of the houses. On their floors were laid like carpets the psychological com-

Left Mies van der Rohe photographed in New York in 1958, the year his Seagram Building, Park Avenue was completed.

Far left László Moholy-Nagy's design for Bauhaus Book 12, *Bauhaus Buildings in Dessau* by Walter Gropius (1930) uses axiometric drawings of state homesteads in Törten across both front and back covers. Bauhaus Archiv, Berlin.

Below Mies van der Rohe's earliest skyscraper designs were for an exhibition project for a building on a site in Friedrichstrasse, Berlin 1921. Bauhaus Archiv, Berlin.

Right Mies' design for the New National Gallery of Art, Berlin, built between 1965/68. Built in steel and glass it provides elegant and light hanging space consisting of a ground floor exhibition area and basement galleries.

Below Mies van der Rohe's design for the German Pavilion at the 1929 World's Fair in Barcelona. Museum of Modern Art, New York, Mies van der Rohe Archive. The Barcelona Pavilion became the prototype for later buildings of this type. The interior and exterior fittings, from the Barcelona chairs to the heating pipes were designed with Mies' customary attention to detail.

Left Mies van der Rohe's model for a glass skyscraper of 1922 is an early example of Mies' radical use of the glass 'disappearing wall', using a skeleton construction rather than loadbearing exterior walls. Museum of Modern Art, New York, Mies van der Rohe Archive.

plexes of young girls. Art stifled life everywhere ... It is a crime to offer young people, who have to be designers in the society of tomorrow, the stale feed of yesterday's art theories as provisions on their way ... The advancing proletarianization of the Institute seemed to us to be in accordance with our times, and the Director was a comrade among comrades.

Meyer ended his letter, 'I see through it all. I understand nothing.' A condition of Meyer's dismissal was that all known communists among the students should depart with him. Some of these formed a design collective with Meyer which offered its services to the Soviet Union, where Meyer was to remain for the next six years. He

was succeeded as Director by the more neutral political figure of Mies van der Rohe, who had declined Gropius' offer of the post in 1928. As with so many aspects of Bauhaus life in its last years, the decision is puzzling. The school was now in a dangerous position, attacked by the left for the dismissal of Meyer and his methods and, increasingly, by the right in these last years of the Weimar Republic of which the Bauhaus was such a quintessential part.

The Wall Street Crash of 'Black Friday', October 24 1929, and the resulting world economic crisis affected all areas of German economic life, including the Bauhaus, as German industry was so heavily indebted

Right László Moholy Nagy's design for his own Bauhaus Book 8 *Painting, Photograph, Film*, 1925. Bauhaus Archiv, Berlin.

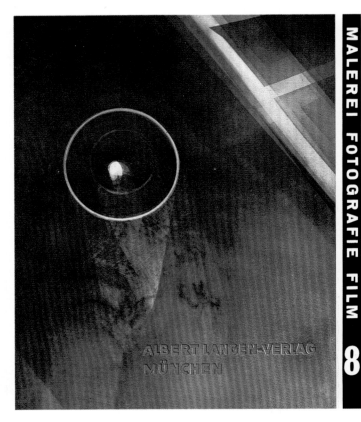

Below Mies van der Rohe's Chicago, Illinois buildings include Lake Shore Drive apartments, built between 1949/51. Mies emigrated to the United States in 1938, becoming Head of the Architecture Department at the Illinois Institute of Technology, Chicago, where he designed several of the Institute buildings as well as domestic apartments.

to American investment. The economic viability of the Bauhaus, which had begun to appear more secure in Meyer's time, began once more to seem shaky and dependent on keeping a politically neutral profile. In Dessau the right wing was becoming more powerful, and there was increasing pressure on Mayor Hesse and the City Council to bring an end to the Bauhaus

Edelbolshewisten, which can be roughly translated as 'high-toned Bolsheviks'. A particular focus for right-wing criticism was the Torten estate on the outskirts of Dessau, which had been begun in Gropius' time and completed in Meyer's. The speed of completion of these 'national homesteads' for working families, together with the radical building methods employed, had led to faults developing which added fuel to right-wing bias against the development and its developers. The estate was viciously attacked in the right-wing press, which called for an end to all 'Judaeo-Christian desert architecture'. The use of such terminology is depressingly similar to that employed in the last days at Weimar to describe the experimental Haus am Horn.

Mies van der Rohe (1880-1969) was an architect of international fame, with a reputation for elegant, spare buildings of glass and steel – his own dictum 'less is more' perfectly describes his work. Left-wing students at the Bauhaus opposed his appointment because of his association with bourgeois housing projects, such as the radical Weissenhof housing development built near Stuttgart in 1927, and his designs for luxurious furniture such as the Weissenhof chair, designed for the estate houses, and the Barcelona chair, designed for the marble, steel and glass German Pavilion built to his own design at the Barcelona World Fair. Such was the strength of protest at Mies' appointment that police were called in to the school and it was closed for several weeks. The radical students were expelled and those remaining were compelled to sign a statement giving up any kind of political activity. The canteen, which had been the center of social life in the first days of the Bauhaus at Weimar, was now seen as the most likely arena for political disturbance. Students had to swear to stay in the canteen 'for no longer than the meal lasts, and not to stay in the canteen in the evening'. There were also regulations about dress codes; students had to appear in Dessau 'well dressed'. Many students left. It is a measure of the Bauhaus' vulnerability at this time that such measures were introduced, and it also signifies the huge gulf between the last days of the Bauhaus and its beginnings in 1919.

Under Mies' direction, the stress laid on architecture became even greater than under Meyer. The workshops became subsidiary, production slowed and the work of the school was further rationalized to just two areas, those of exterior building and interior design. The latter department was run under the direction of Lili Reich (1885-1947), Mies' closest associate. The students concentrated their efforts almost exclusively on individual dwellings, working very directly to principles laid down by Mies in his own architecture. As a result the work of many of the students at this time tends to replicate their Professor's. Many drawings of interiors, for example the 'single-story residence with patio' project, bear clone-like similarity to Mies' designs, even to their glass screen-walls and ritual placing of two Barcelona or Weissenhof chairs.

The students' respect for their Director's work is understandable, as Mies was already considered to be one of the most distinguished architects of the modern movement. In 1927 he had been made director of the ambitious Weissenhof Exhibition estate, sponsored by the Werkbund to explore the theme of *Wohnung* (the dwelling) with contributions by most of the leading European architects of the day, including Peter Behrens, J J P Oud, Mart Stam, Gropius and Le Corbusier. Mies contributed the design for the apartment block which crowned the site.

Son of a master mason, Ludwig Mies (van der Rohe was added in 1913) was employed by Peter Behrens as job architect on the German Embassy building in St Petersburg between 1908-12 and became well-known for the elegant minimalism of his glass and steel architecture. Like Gropius, whose architectural career is similar in certain respects, Mies was a member of the radical Novembergruppe, acting as its exhibition director between 1922-25. Mies, like Gropius earlier in his career, designed a radical memorial to left-wing heroes – in Mies' case the monument to Rosa Luxembourg and Karl Liebknecht in Berlin in 1926. This took the form of a Cubist-inspired, blood-red brick wall constructed at the grave of the two martyrs in Berlin. The memorial, which was surmounted by a huge metal star with hammer and sickle, was the focus of many Nazi demonstrations and was subsequently destroyed beyond hope of restoration, unlike Gropius' equivalent memorial, the Monument to the March Dead in Weimar.

By the time Mies became Director of the Bauhaus, he was concerned to present a 'safe' political profile for the sake of the survival of the school, which had at all costs to appear politically neutral, but the political situation in Germany now made such efforts increasingly irrelevant. In November 1931, the Nazis made significant gains in the Dessau elections. The following August a crucial motion to close the Bauhaus was carried in the City Council, although its fate had been sealed the month before when an inspection tour of the Bauhaus had been carried out by National Socialist representatives. The Dessau newspaper *Anhalter Tageszeitung* of July 1932 concluded its report of the inspection with the following declaration:

The disappearance of this so-called 'Institute of Design' will mean the disappearance from German soil of one of the most prominent places of Jewish-Marxist 'art' manifestation. May the total demolition follow and may on the same ground where today stands the somber glass palace of oriental taste,

the 'aquarium' as it has been popularly dubbed in Dessau, soon rise homesteads and parks that will provide German people with homes and places for relaxation. 'The robe has fallen, the Duke must follow'.

The Dessau Bauhaus was closed on September 30 1932. That the buildings were not razed to the ground is a measure of the groundswell of public opinion in Europe against the school's closure. The great glass wall was later bricked in, an ironic tribute to its powerful symbolism, and the building allowed to decay until its restoration thirty years later. In a final gesture Mies removed his students to Berlin, where classes were hastily resumed in a former telephone factory in the suburb of Steglitz. The school operated for the next few months as a private institution on funds from well-wishers and on the income still generated by Bauhaus products – the copyrights to the wallpaper designs were particularly valuable. Four months later, on January 30 1933, Hitler became Chancellor, and on April 11, as the student Pius E Pahl reported:

Early in the morning police arrived with trucks and closed the Bauhaus. Bauhaus members without proper identification (and who had this?) were loaded on the trucks and taken away.

Above The Berlin Bauhaus, housed in a disused telephone factory with student Ernst Louis Beck in the foreground. Bauhaus Archiv, Berlin.

Epilogue

After the events of April 11 1933 it was obvious that the Bauhaus could not continue, and on July 22 the remaining members of the Faculty voted its dissolution. A general exodus of staff had started at the time of Gropius' departure; Klee and Gunta Stölzl had been the latest to leave in 1931, with Kandinsky and Albers the only surviving Masters to see the end. Thanks largely to Gropius' efforts to promote the Bauhaus internationally since its foundation, however, staff and students were welcomed as educators abroad when pressures from within Germany forced them to emigrate, particularly as they were perceived as victims of Nazi oppression. Those who wished to stay and work in Germany found themselves gradually prevented from earning their living. Works by Feininger, Itten, Kandinsky, Klee, Bayer, Marcks, Muche, Moholy-Nagy and Schlemmer were included in the notorious 'Degenerate Art' touring exhibition of 1937-38, which further sealed the artists' fate. Klee and Itten returned to their native Switzerland, Feininger returned to America fifty years after leaving it, Kandinsky left for Paris, Muche and Schlemmer joined Gerhard Marcks at the paint factory owned by Kurt Herberts in Wuppertal which served to provide employment and a refuge at this time.

By far the most significant exodus of Bauhaus staff was to the United States. Gropius himself arrived there to become Chairman of the Graduate School of Design at Harvard in 1937, where Breuer was to join him for a period in the spreading of Bauhaus ideas. Gropius first set up an architectural practice in England, where several projects, including the Impington Village College in Cambridgeshire, were built in partnership with the English architect Maxwell Fry. *New Architecture and the Bauhaus* was published in England in 1935, and there were plans for Gropius to teach at the Royal College of Art. But it was in America that Gropius' ideas were to have the greatest impact. In May 1953 he wrote

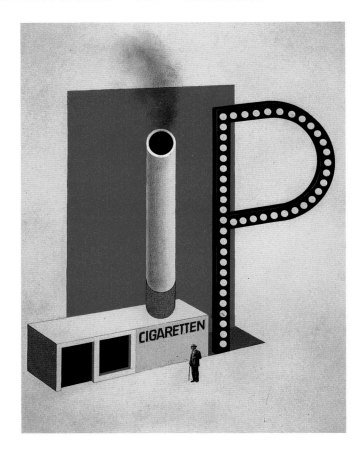

to Fritz Hesse, who had been reinstated as Mayor of Dessau after the war:

When you live in Germany you can hardly imagine how world famous the Bauhaus has become, especially in the United States and England. In both countries the teaching curriculum of the schools of art and architecture have followed the teachings of the Bauhaus . . . and the official state examination for architects contains the obligatory question 'What is the Bauhaus?' Therefore it was all worthwhile, though neither you nor I knew beforehand the great and almost insurmountable difficulties we were going to have.

Above right Herbert Bayer's design for a cigarette kiosk, 1924. Bauhaus Archiv, Berlin © DACS 1991. The size of the projected building can be judged by the scale figure. The chimney was intended to emit smoke.

Right Wassily Kandinsky *Jocular Sounds*, 1929, oil on cardboard, 13½ × 19 inches (34.9 × 48.9cm). The Busch-Reisinger Museum, Harvard University, © ADAGP Paris and DACS London 1991.

Bayer emigrated in 1938 and assisted Gropius in the organization of the New York Museum of Modern Art exhibition of that year, which did so much to spread Bauhaus ideas to a wider public. Mies emigrated in 1937, taking up the directorship of the Illinois Institute of Technology in Chicago in 1938. The elegant Neue Nationalgalerie (designed in 1965) in Berlin, which houses that city's finest collection of modern art, is his monument in the city for which his first glass skyscrapers were designed forty years before and in which he tried to ensure the continuation of the Bauhaus.

Josef and Anni Albers worked at Black Mountain College, North Carolina from 1933 until 1959, when Josef became Chairman of the Department of Design at Yale. He developed the ideas of his *Vorkurs* here and exerted a powerful influence on his students, both through his teachings and the development of his *Homage to the Square* series of paintings. Anni Albers' influential text *On Weaving* was published in 1965, enhancing her already influential reputation.

However widely disseminated Bauhaus ideas were to become in the years following its dissolution, its formal heir was the New Bauhaus in Chicago, set up under Moholy-Nagy's directorship in 1937 with Gropius as consultant. Financial difficulties saw its dissolution a year later, but the indefatigable Moholy reopened the institution with the new title of School of Design in 1939, backing it from his own financial resources as a design consultant and modifying its teaching programme (which included evening classes) from the ambitious plans first conceived for the New Bauhaus. Moholy continued to direct the Institute until his death from leukaemia at the age of 51 in 1946, presiding over its success as a major force in American industrial design while continuing his own prolific work which included the design of the Parker 51 pen. Gropius wrote in his obituary tribute:

We might call the scope of his contribution 'Leonardian' so versatile and colorful has it been. He was successful at once as a thinker and as an inventor, as a writer and as a teacher.

Above left Berlin Vase by William Wagenfeld. Courtesy of Barry Friedmann Ltd. His wide ranging work in a variety of materials shows the typical versatility of the Bauhaus student.

Above Wilhelm Wagenfeld and Karl Jucker's table lamp of 1923. Bauhaus Archiv, Berlin.

Left Ruth Hollos-Consemüller's gobelin of about 1926 uses the simple geometric shapes and clear primary colors so characteristic of the work of the weaving workshop at this time. Bauhaus Archiv, Berlin.

In 1968 at the London opening of the 'The Bauhaus: 50 Years' exhibition, designed by Bayer, Gropius' opening address dealt with what he perceived as a misunderstanding of Bauhaus work which might be said to persist over twenty years later:

... It was described as a simple-minded, purely utilitarian approach to design, devoid of an imagination that would give grace and beauty to life.

His characteristic idealism still in evidence, Gropius continued:

The slowly developed attitude in the Bauhaus to *in*clude everything and *ex*clude nothing which belongs to the totality of life, to say 'and' instead of 'either/or' has anticipated today's comeback to a total involvement as against narrow specialization.

In this last decade of the twentieth century, in the new Europe, in the United States and in Japan (where interest in the Bauhaus has been a growing phenomenon for some years), there is a new interest both in the pluralism of Gropius' approach and its idealism. The artists and designers of the future begin their studies with diagnostic foundation courses which spring directly from the *Vorkurs* — perhaps the most lasting of Bauhaus legacies. The fabric of all our lives is affected by the Bauhaus; we live and work in buildings influenced by its ideas, and use everyday objects such as reading lamps and chairs which had their origins in the workshops at Dessau. Interest in the Bauhaus has never been greater, especially among the young; the Gropius-designed Bauhaus Archiv in Berlin is busy

with visitors from all over the world, who come to see the cult objects of the Bauhaus years, from Gunta Stölzl's tapestries to the working model of Moholy's dynamic *Light-Space Modulator*. The Bauhaus neatly encapsulates the idea of the *Zeitgeist* or spirit of the age. Its lifespan was exactly that of the Weimar Republic, to which it was inextricably bound. The Bauhaus was born in the same city as the Republic, mirrored the ideas and brilliance of that extraordinary time and, like the Weimar Republic, met its end in Berlin.

Above Marianne Brandt's silver teapot with ebony handles, designed in 1924. Courtesy of the Trustees of the British Museum.

Opposite Marianne Brandt's versatility is typical of the Bauhaus student, especially those, like her, who became Young Masters. Her ironic photocollage *The Rebirth of Beauty* dates from 1927. Bauhaus Archiv, Berlin.

Left The original building of the Chicago Bauhaus, photograph taken in 1937. The inscription above the door reads 'the new bauhaus, AMERICAN SCHOOL OF DESIGN.'

Index

Figures in **bold** refer to the main treatment of a subject; figures in *italic* refer to illustrations.

Acknowledgements

The publishers would like to thank Martin Bristow, who designed this book; Jill Ford, who indexed it; Sabine Hartmann of the Bauhaus Archiv; and Jessica Orebi Gann, the project editor. We would also like to thank the institutions, agencies and individuals listed for providing illustrative material.

Architectural Association, London, Slide Library: pages 18 (below), 112 (below)

Architectural Press: page 121 (top)

Badisches Landesmuseum Karlsruhe Bildarchiv: page 47 (bottom)

Baltimore Museum of Art, Alan and Janet Wurtzburger Collection: page 60

Barry Friedman Ltd, New York: pages 19, 63 (top left), 74, 77 (left), 105 (bottom), 120, 171 (top left)

Bauhaus Archiv, Berlin: pages 2, 9, 10 (top), 16, 17 (bottom), 18 (top), 20, 22, 23, (bottom), 24 (bottom), 25 (both), 28 (bottom), 29 (both), 30 (bottom), 31 (both), 32 (all three), 33 (both), 34, 37 (bottom), 38 (top), 39, 40 (both), 41 (both), 43 (bottom), 46, 47 (top), 48 (both), 51 (top left and right), 52 (top), 54, 58, 61, 62 (bottom), 63 (top right and bottom), 65, 69/photo courtesy Lucia Moholy, 70, 72, 75 (top), 76 (top), 77 (right), 78 (bottom), 80, 81 (both), 82, 84, 85 (both), 86 (top left and right), 87, 88, 89 (top), 90, 92, 93 (bottom), 94 (both), 95 (both), 96 (bottom), 97, 98, 99, 100, 103 (both), 104 (both), 105 (top), 107 (bottom), 108, 111 (both), 112 (top), 113 (both), 114 (both), 116, 118 (bottom), 119, 122 (bottom), 124, 127, 128, 131 (bottom), 132 (both), 133 (all three), 134 (all three), 135 (all three), 136, 139 (both), 140 (bottom), 142 (top), 143, 148 (top three), 152 (bottom), 153, 154 (top), 155 (top right), 157 (top), 160 (both), 161 (both), 162 (both), 163 (bottom), 166 (top), 167, 170 (top), 171 (top right and bottom), 172

Bildarchiv Preussischer Kulturbesitz, Berlin: Page 42

British Museum, courtesy of the Trustees: pages 15 (both) 24 (top), 36, 37 (top), 86 (bottom), 107 (top right), 110, 130, 150 (bottom), 173 (top)

The Busch-Reisinger Museum, Harvard University: page 38/purchase in memory of Edna K Loeb, 43 (top)/Kuno Francke Memorial Fund and Association Fund, 107 (top left)/gift of Sybil Moholy-Nagy, 154 (bottom), 170 (bottom)

Centraal Museum, Utrecht: page 93 (top)

Cologne Institute for Theatrical Studies: page 115 (bottom right)

Germanisches Nationalmuseum Nürnberg: page 79 (bottom)

Hamburg Kunsthalle: page 151 (top)

Angelo Hornak: page 166 (bottom)

Hunterian Art Gallery, University of Glasgow, Mackintosh Collection: pages 13 (top), 14

Kuntsgewerbe Sammlung Stadt Bieldfeld: page 79 (top)

Kuntsammlungen zu Weimar: pages 1, 11, 12 (top), 28 (top), 30 (top), 44, 49 (both), 50, 51 (bottom), 52 (bottom), 53 (both), 55, 73 (bottom), 76 (bottom), 78 (top), 89 (bottom), 118 (top), 121, 122 (top left and right), 123 (both), 131 (top), 141 (bottom), 142 (bottom)

Metropolitan Museum of Art, New York, Bergruen Klee Collection, 1984: pages 26, 62 (top)

Museum of Modern Art, New York: pages 23 (top)/acquired through the Lillie P Bliss bequest, 148 (bottom)/gift of Lily Auchinloss, 164 (bottom)/Mies van der Rohe Archive, 165/Mies van der Rohe Archive

Museum of Modern Art, Oxford: page 141 (top)

Photoarchiv C Raman Schlemmer: pages 64 (both), 146, 149 (both), 150 (top left and bottom right), 151 (bottom right), 152 (top), 155 (top left and bottom right), 156 (both), 157 (bottom)

Prentenkabinett der Rijksuniversiteit Leiden: page 56

Rheinisches Bildarchiv: page 17 (top)

Royal Academy of Arts, London: page 102

San Francisco Museum of Modern Art: 106/gift of Anni Albers and the Josef Albers Foundation

The Solomon R Guggenheim Museum, New York: page 2, 67

Stedelijk Museum, Amsterdam: pages 66, 140 (top),

Stuart Windsor: page 115 (bottom),

Tate Gallery, London: page 59

Thyssen-Bornemisza Foundation, Lugano: page 27

University of East Anglia Collection/photo Michael Brandon-Jones: page 158

UPI/Bettmann Archive: pages 10 (bottom), 96 (top), 115 (top), 163 (top), 168, 173 (bottom)

Victoria and Albert Museum, London: pages 12 (bottom), 73 (top), 75 (bottom), 125 (bottom), 126 (all three), 144, 145 (both)

William Morris Gallery, London: page 13 (bottom)